GENOCIDE **&** PERSECUTION

| East Pakistan

Titles in the Genocide and Persecution Series

GENOCIDE & PERSECUTION

| East Pakistan

Noah Berlatsky
Book Editor

Frank Chalk
Consulting Editor

GREENHAVEN PRESS
A part of Gale, Cengage Learning

 GALE
CENGAGE Learning·

Detroit • New York • San Francisco • New Haven, Conn • Waterville, Maine • London

Elizabeth Des Chenes, *Director, Publishing Solutions*

© 2013 Greenhaven Press, a part of Gale, Cengage Learning

Gale and Greenhaven Press are registered trademarks used herein under license.

For more information, contact:
Greenhaven Press
27500 Drake Rd.
Farmington Hills, MI 48331-3535
Or you can visit our Internet site at gale.cengage.com.

For product information and technology assistance, contact us at:

Gale Customer Support, 1-800-877-4253
For permission to use material from this text or product, submit all requests online at www.cengage.com/permissions

Further permissions questions can be emailed to permissionrequest@cengage.com

Every effort is made to ensure that Greenhaven Press accurately reflects the original intent of the authors. Every effort has been made to trace the owners of copyrighted material.

Cover image © Bettmann/Corbis.
Interior barbed wire artwork © f9photos, used under license from Shutterstock.com.

LIBRARY OF CONGRESS CATALOGING-IN-PUBLICATION DATA

East Pakistan / Noah Berlatsky, book editor.
   p. cm. -- (Genocide and persecution)
   Includes bibliographical references and index.
   ISBN 978-0-7377-6256-3 (hardcover)
   1. Bangladesh--History--Revolution, 1971--Atrocities. 2. Genocide--Bangladesh--History--20th century. I. Berlatsky, Noah.
   DS395.5.E27 2012
   954.9205'14--dc23
                                           2012014595

Printed in the United States of America
1 2 3 4 5 6 7 16 15 14 13 12

Contents

Preface

"For the dead and the living, we must bear witness."

Elie Wiesel, Nobel laureate and Holocaust survivor

The histories of many nations are shaped by horrific events involving torture, violent repression, and systematic mass killings. The inhumanity of such events is difficult to comprehend, yet understanding why such events take place, what impact they have on society, and how they may be prevented in the future is vitally important. The Genocide and Persecution series provides readers with anthologies of previously published materials on acts of genocide, crimes against humanity, and other instances of extreme persecution, with an emphasis on events taking place in the twentieth and twenty-first centuries. The series offers essential historical background on these significant events in modern world history, presents the issues and controversies surrounding the events, and provides first-person narratives from people whose lives were altered by the events. By providing primary sources, as well as analysis of crucial issues, these volumes help develop critical-thinking skills and support global connections. In addition, the series directly addresses curriculum standards focused on informational text and literary nonfiction and explicitly promotes literacy in history and social studies.

Each Genocide and Persecution volume focuses on genocide, crimes against humanity, or severe persecution. Material from a variety of primary and secondary sources presents a multinational perspective on the event. Articles are carefully edited and introduced to provide context for readers. The series includes volumes on significant and widely studied events like the Holocaust, as well as events that are less often studied, such as the East Pakistan genocide in what is now Bangladesh. Some volumes focus on multiple events endured by a specific people, such as the Kurds, or multiple events enacted over time by a particular oppressor or in a particular location, such as the People's Republic of China.

Each volume is organized into three chapters. The first chapter provides readers with general background information and uses primary sources such as testimony from tribunals or international courts, documents or speeches from world leaders, and legislative text. The second chapter presents multinational perspectives on issues and controversies and addresses current implications or long-lasting effects of the event. Viewpoints explore such topics as root causes; outside interventions, if any; the impact on the targeted group and the region; and the contentious issues that arose in the aftermath. The third chapter presents first-person narratives from affected people, including survivors, family members of victims, perpetrators, officials, aid workers, and other witnesses.

In addition, numerous features are included in each volume of Genocide and Persecution:

- An annotated **table of contents** provides a brief summary of each essay in the volume.
- A **foreword** gives important background information on the recognition, definition, and study of genocide in recent history and examines current efforts focused on the prevention of future atrocities.
- A **chronology** offers important dates leading up to, during, and following the event.
- **Primary sources**—including historical newspaper accounts, testimony, and personal narratives—are among the varied selections in the anthology.
- **Illustrations**—including a world map, photographs, charts, graphs, statistics, and tables—are closely tied

to the text and chosen to help readers understand key points or concepts.

- **Sidebars**—including biographies of key figures and overviews of earlier or related historical events—offer additional content.
- **Pedagogical features**—including analytical exercises, writing prompts, and group activities—introduce each chapter and help reinforce the material. These features promote proficiency in writing, speaking, and listening skills and literacy in history and social studies.
- A **glossary** defines key terms, as needed.
- An annotated list of international **organizations to contact** presents sources of additional information on the volume topic.
- A **list of primary source documents** provides an annotated list of reports, treaties, resolutions, and judicial decisions related to the volume topic.
- A **for further research** section offers a bibliography of books, periodical articles, and Internet sources and an annotated section of other items such as films and websites.
- A comprehensive subject **index** provides access to key people, places, events, and subjects cited in the text.

The Genocide and Persecution series illuminates atrocities that cannot and should not be forgotten. By delving deeply into these events from a variety of perspectives, students and other readers are provided with the information they need to think critically about the past and its implications for the future.

Foreword

The term *genocide* often appears in news stories and other literature. It is not widely known, however, that the core meaning of the term comes from a legal definition, and the concept became part of international criminal law only in 1951 when the United Nations Convention on the Prevention and Punishment of the Crime of Genocide came into force. The word *genocide* appeared in print for the first time in 1944 when Raphael Lemkin, a Polish Jewish refugee from Adolf Hitler's World War II invasion of Eastern Europe, invented the term and explored its meaning in his pioneering book *Axis Rule in Occupied Europe*.

Humanity's Recognition of Genocide and Persecution

Lemkin understood that throughout the history of the human race there have always been leaders who thought they could solve their problems not only through victory in war, but also by destroying entire national, ethnic, racial, or religious groups. Such annihilations of entire groups, in Lemkin's view, deprive the world of the very cultural diversity and richness in languages, traditions, values, and practices that distinguish the human race from all other life on earth. Genocide is not only unjust, it threatens the very existence and progress of human civilization, in Lemkin's eyes.

Looking to the past, Lemkin understood that the prevailing coarseness and brutality of earlier human societies and the lower value placed on human life obscured the existence of genocide. Sacrifice and exploitation, as well as torture and public execution, had been common at different times in history. Looking toward a more humane future, Lemkin asserted the need to punish—and when possible prevent—a crime for which there had been no name until he invented it.

Legal Definitions of Genocide

On December 9, 1948, the United Nations adopted its Convention on the Prevention and Punishment of the Crime of Genocide (UNGC). Under Article II, genocide

> means any of the following acts committed with intent to destroy, in whole or in part, a national, ethnical, racial or religious group, as such:
>
> (a) Killing members of the group;
>
> (b) Causing serious bodily or mental harm to members of the group;
>
> (c) Deliberately inflicting on the group conditions of life calculated to bring about its physical destruction in whole or in part;
>
> (d) Imposing measures intended to prevent births within the group;
>
> (e) Forcibly transferring children of the group to another group.

Article III of the convention defines the elements of the crime of genocide, making punishable:

> (a) Genocide;
>
> (b) Conspiracy to commit genocide;
>
> (c) Direct and public incitement to commit genocide;
>
> (d) Attempt to commit genocide;
>
> (e) Complicity in genocide.

After intense debate, the architects of the convention excluded acts committed with intent to destroy social, political, and economic groups from the definition of genocide. Thus, attempts to destroy whole social classes—the physically and mentally challenged, and homosexuals, for example—are not acts of genocide under the terms of the UNGC. These groups achieved a belated but very significant measure of protection under international criminal law in the Rome Statute of the International Criminal

Court, adopted at a conference on July 17, 1998, and entered into force on July 1, 2002.

The Rome Statute defined a crime against humanity in the following way:

> any of the following acts when committed as part of a wide-spread and systematic attack directed against any civilian population:
>
> (a) Murder;
>
> (b) Extermination;
>
> (c) Enslavement;
>
> (d) Deportation or forcible transfer of population;
>
> (e) Imprisonment or other severe deprivation of physical liberty in violation of fundamental rules of international law;
>
> (f) Torture;
>
> (g) Rape, sexual slavery, enforced prostitution, forced pregnancy, enforced sterilization, or any other form of sexual violence of comparable gravity;
>
> (h) Persecution against any identifiable group or collectivity on political, racial, national, ethnic, cultural, religious, gender . . . or other grounds that are universally recognized as impermissible under international law, in connection with any act referred to in this paragraph or any crime within the jurisdiction of this Court;
>
> (i) Enforced disappearance of persons;
>
> (j) The crime of apartheid;
>
> (k) Other inhumane acts of a similar character intentionally causing great suffering, or serious injury to body or to mental or physical health.

Although genocide is often ranked as "the crime of crimes," in practice prosecutors find it much easier to convict perpetrators of crimes against humanity rather than genocide under domestic laws. However, while Article I of the UNGC declares that countries adhering to the UNGC recognize genocide as "a crime under international law which they undertake to prevent and to punish," the Rome Statute provides no comparable international mechanism for the prosecution of crimes against humanity. A treaty would help individual countries and international institutions introduce measures to prevent crimes against humanity, as well as open more avenues to the domestic and international prosecution of war criminals.

The Evolving Laws of Genocide

In the aftermath of the serious crimes committed against civilians in the former Yugoslavia since 1991 and the Rwanda genocide of 1994, the United Nations Security Council created special international courts to bring the alleged perpetrators of these events to justice. While the UNGC stands as the standard definition of genocide in law, the new courts contributed significantly to today's nuanced meaning of genocide, crimes against humanity, ethnic cleansing, and serious war crimes in international criminal law.

Also helping to shape contemporary interpretations of such mass atrocity crimes are the special and mixed courts for Sierra Leone, Cambodia, Lebanon, and Iraq, which may be the last of their type in light of the creation of the International Criminal Court (ICC), with its broad jurisdiction over mass atrocity crimes in all countries that adhere to the Rome Statute of the ICC. The Yugoslavia and Rwanda tribunals have already clarified the law of genocide, ruling that rape can be prosecuted as a weapon in committing genocide, evidence of intent can be absent when convicting low-level perpetrators of genocide, and public incitement to commit genocide is a crime even if genocide does not immediately follow the incitement.

Several current controversies about genocide are worth noting and will require more research in the future:

1. Dictators accused of committing genocide or persecution may hold onto power more tightly for fear of becoming

vulnerable to prosecution after they step down. Therefore, do threats of international indictments of these alleged perpetrators actually delay transfers of power to more representative rulers, thereby causing needless suffering?

2. Would the large sum of money spent for international retributive justice be better spent on projects directly benefiting the survivors of genocide and persecution?

3. Can international courts render justice impartially or do they deliver only "victors' justice," that is the application of one set of rules to judge the vanquished and a different and laxer set of rules to judge the victors?

It is important to recognize that the law of genocide is constantly evolving, and scholars searching for the roots and early warning signs of genocide may prefer to use their own definitions of genocide in their work. While the UNGC stands as the standard definition of genocide in law, the debate over its interpretation and application will never end. The ultimate measure of the value of any definition of genocide is its utility for identifying the roots of genocide and preventing future genocides.

Motives for Genocide and Early Warning Signs

When identifying past cases of genocide, many scholars work with some version of the typology of motives published in 1990 by historian Frank Chalk and sociologist Kurt Jonassohn in their book *The History and Sociology of Genocide*. The authors identify the following four motives and acknowledge that they may overlap, or several lesser motives might also drive a perpetrator:

1. To eliminate a real or potential threat, as in Imperial Rome's decision to annihilate Carthage in 146 BC.

2. To spread terror among real or potential enemies, as in Genghis Khan's destruction of city-states and people who rebelled against the Mongols in the thirteenth century.

3. To acquire economic wealth, as in the case of the Massachusetts Puritans' annihilation of the native Pequot people in 1637.

4. To implement a belief, theory, or an ideology, as in the case of Germany's decision under Hitler and the Nazis to destroy completely the Jewish people of Europe from 1941 to 1945.

Although these motives represent differing goals, they share common early warning signs of genocide. A good example of genocide in recent times that could have been prevented through close attention to early warning signs was the genocide of 1994 inflicted on the people labeled as "Tutsi" in Rwanda. Between 1959 and 1963, the predominantly Hutu political parties in power stigmatized all Tutsi as members of a hostile racial group, violently forcing their leaders and many civilians into exile in neighboring countries through a series of assassinations and massacres. Despite systematic exclusion of Tutsi from service in the military, government security agencies, and public service, as well as systematic discrimination against them in higher education, hundreds of thousands of Tutsi did remain behind in Rwanda. Government-issued cards identified each Rwandan as Hutu or Tutsi.

A generation later, some Tutsi raised in refugee camps in Uganda and elsewhere joined together, first organizing politically and then militarily, to reclaim a place in their homeland. When the predominantly Tutsi Rwanda Patriotic Front invaded Rwanda from Uganda in October 1990, extremist Hutu political parties demonized all of Rwanda's Tutsi as traitors, ratcheting up hate propaganda through radio broadcasts on government-run Radio Rwanda and privately owned radio station RTLM. Within the print media, *Kangura* and other publications used vicious cartoons to further demonize Tutsi and to stigmatize any Hutu who dared advocate bringing Tutsi into the government. Massacres of dozens and later hundreds of Tutsi sprang up even as Rwandans prepared to elect a coalition government led by moderate political parties, and as the United Nations dispatched a small international military force led by Canadian general Roméo Dallaire to oversee the elections and political transition. Late in 1992, an international human rights organization's investigating team detected the hate propaganda campaign, verified systematic massacres of Tutsi, and warned the international community that Rwanda had already entered the early stages of genocide, to no avail. On April 6, 1994, Rwanda's genocidal killing accelerated at an alarming pace when someone shot down the airplane flying Rwandan president Juvenal Habyarimana home from peace talks in Arusha, Tanzania.

Hundreds of thousands of Tutsi civilians—including children, women, and the elderly—died horrible deaths because the world ignored the early warning signs of the genocide and refused to act. Prominent among those early warning signs were: 1) systematic, government-decreed discrimination against the Tutsi as members of a supposed racial group; 2) government-issued identity cards labeling every Tutsi as a member of a racial group; 3) hate propaganda casting all Tutsi as subversives and traitors; 4) organized assassinations and massacres targeting Tutsi; and 5) indoctrination of militias and special military units to believe that all Tutsi posed a genocidal threat to the existence of Hutu and would enslave Hutu if they ever again became the rulers of Rwanda.

Genocide Prevention and the Responsibility to Protect

The shock waves emanating from the Rwanda genocide forced world leaders at least to acknowledge in principle that the national sovereignty of offending nations cannot trump the responsibility of those governments to prevent the infliction of mass atrocities on their own people. When governments violate that obligation, the member states of the United Nations have a responsibility to get involved. Such involvement can take the form of, first, offering to help the local government change its ways through technical advice and development aid, and second—if the local government persists in assaulting its own people—initiating armed intervention to protect the civilians at risk. In 2005 the United Nations began to implement the Responsibility to Protect initiative, a framework of principles to guide the international community in preventing mass atrocities.

As in many real-world domains, theory and practice often diverge. Genocide and crimes against humanity are rooted in problems that produce failing states: poverty, poor education, extreme nationalism, lawlessness, dictatorship, and corruption. Implementing the principles of the Responsibility to Protect doctrine burdens intervening state leaders with the necessity of addressing each of those problems over a long period of time. And when those problems prove too intractable and complex to solve easily, the citizens of the intervening nations may lose patience, voting out the leader who initiated the intervention. Arguments based solely on humanitarian principles fail to overcome such concerns. What is needed to persuade political leaders to stop preventable mass atrocities are compelling arguments based on their own national interests.

Preventable mass atrocities threaten the national interests of all states in five specific ways:

1. Mass atrocities create conditions that engender widespread and concrete threats from terrorism, piracy, and other forms of lawlessness on the land and sea;
2. Mass atrocities facilitate the spread of warlordism, whose tentacles block affordable access to vital raw materials produced in the affected country and threaten the prosperity of all nations that depend on the consumption of these resources;
3. Mass atrocities trigger cascades of refugees and internally displaced populations that, combined with climate change and growing international air travel, will accelerate the

worldwide incidence of lethal infectious diseases;

4. Mass atrocities spawn single-interest parties and political agendas that drown out more diverse political discourse in the countries where the atrocities take place and in the countries that host large numbers of refugees. Xenophobia and nationalist backlashes are the predictable consequences of government indifference to mass atrocities elsewhere that could have been prevented through early actions;

5. Mass atrocities foster the spread of national and transnational criminal networks trafficking in drugs, women, arms, contraband, and laundered money.

Alerting elected political representatives to the consequences of mass atrocities should be part of every student movement's agenda in the twenty-first century. Adam Smith, the great political economist and author of *The Wealth of Nations*, put it best when he wrote: "It is not from the benevolence of the butcher, the brewer, or the baker that we expect our dinner, but from their regard to their own interest." Self-interest is a powerful engine for good in the marketplace and can be an equally powerful motive and source of inspiration for state action to prevent genocide and mass persecution. In today's new global village, the lives we save may be our own.

Frank Chalk

Frank Chalk, who has a doctorate from the University of Wisconsin-Madison, is a professor of history and director of the Montreal Institute for Genocide and Human Rights Studies at Concordia University in Montreal, Canada. He is coauthor, with Kurt

Jonassohn, of The History and Sociology of Genocide *(1990); coauthor with General Roméo Dallaire, Kyle Matthews, Carla Barqueiro, and Simon Doyle of* Mobilizing the Will to Intervene: Leadership to Prevent Mass Atrocities *(2010); and associate editor of the three-volume Macmillan Reference USA* Encyclopedia of Genocide and Crimes Against Humanity *(2004). Chalk served as president of the International Association of Genocide Scholars from June 1999 to June 2001. His current research focuses on the use of radio and television broadcasting in the incitement and prevention of genocide, and domestic laws on genocide. For more information on genocide and examples of the experiences of people displaced by genocide and other human rights violations, interested readers can consult the websites of the Montreal Institute for Genocide and Human Rights Studies (http://migs.concordia.ca) and the Montreal Life Stories project (www.lifestoriesmontreal.ca).*

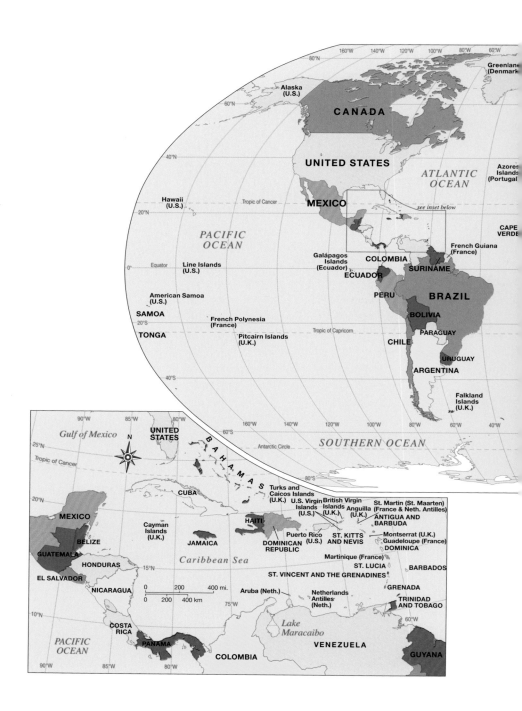

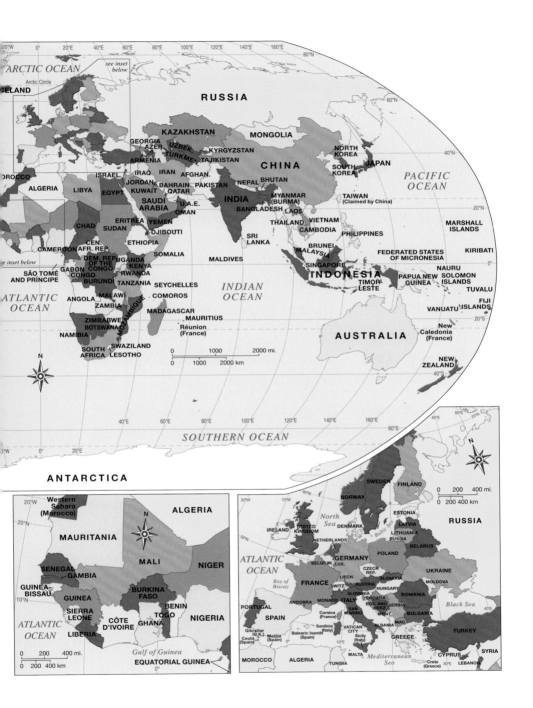

Chronology

August 14, 1947 The British grant independence to their possessions in Asia. Pakistan and India both become independent nations.

February 25, 1948 Urdu is declared the national language of Pakistan.

March 11, 1948 The Bangladesh Language Movement begins as Bangladeshi students strike to protest the fact that Bengali is not a national language of Pakistan.

June 23, 1949 The Awami League political party is formed.

February 21, 1952 Police fire on students agitating for the Bengali language.

February 29, 1956 Bengali becomes one of the national languages of Pakistan.

1966 Sheikh Mujibur Rahman emerges as a leader of the push for East Pakistan autonomy with his Six Point Movement.

1968 The government of Pakistan files charges against Sheikh Mujibur Rahman, accusing him of sedition.

January–February 1969 Mass uprisings and protests sweep through East Pakistan. Pakistan President Ayub Khan resigns and is replaced by Yahya Khan. Mujibur Rahman is acquitted of sedition charges.

December 7, 1970	The first general elections are held in Pakistan. The Awami League gains a majority in Parliament. A political crisis results.
March 7, 1971	Mujibur Rahman makes a historic speech urging East Pakistan to fight for independence.
March 25, 1971	Yahya Khan launches Operation Searchlight, a military action against East Pakistan resulting in numerous atrocities. Mujibur Rahman is arrested.
March 27, 1971	The Bangladesh declaration of independence is broadcast by radio.
December 3, 1971	India enters the war against West Pakistan.
December 16, 1971	Pakistan surrenders to India.
December 20, 1971	Yahya Khan steps down; Zulfikar Ali Bhutto becomes president of Pakistan.
December 16, 1972	The constitution of Bangladesh is established.
March 7, 1972	The first election in Bangladesh is held. Mujibur Rahman's Awami League wins; Rahman becomes Bangladesh's first president.
February 22, 1973	Pakistan recognizes Bangladesh.
April 9, 1973	Bangladesh, India, and Pakistan sign a tripartite agreement on return of hostages, war crimes, and other issues.
August 15, 1975	Sheikh Mujibur Rahman is assassinated.

| November 2011 | Trials of those alleged to have committed war crimes in 1971 begin in Bangladesh. |

CHAPTER 1

Historical Background on the East Pakistan Genocide

Chapter Exercises

STATISTICS

	Bangladesh	Pakistan
Total area	143,998 sq km World ranking: 95	796,095 sq km World ranking: 36
Population	158,570,535 World ranking: 7	187,342,721 World ranking: 6
Ethnic groups	Bengali 98%, other 2% (including tribal groups, non-Bengali Muslims)	Punjabi 44.68%, Pashtun (Pathan) 15.42%, Sindhi 14.1%, Sariaki 8.38%, Muhajirs 7.57%, Balochi 3.57%, other 6.28%
Religions	Muslim 89.5%, Hindu 9.6%, other .9%	Muslim 95% (Sunni 75%, Shia 20%), other (includes Christian and Hindu) 5%
Literacy (total population)	47.9%	49.9%
GDP	$258.6 billion World ranking: 45	$464.9 billion World ranking: 28

Source: *The World Factbook*. Washington, DC: Central Intelligence Agency, 2012. www.cia.gov.

1. Analyzing Statistics

Question 1: Compare the major ethnic groups in Bangladesh to the major ethnic groups in Pakistan. Now compare the major religion in Bangladesh and the major religion in Pakistan. Based on your findings, which do you think was more important in the East Pakistan conflict, religious differences or ethnic differences? Explain your reasoning.

Question 2: Which is larger and by how much: the GDP of Pakistan or the GDP of Bangladesh? In a conflict between the two, which would have more resources? Explain your answer.

Question 3: Compare the populations of Pakistan and Bangladesh. Then look at the ethnic group percentages in both countries. If Pakistan and Bangladesh were one country, would Bengalis, Pashtuns, or Punjabis be the largest ethnic group in that combined country? Based on your answers, explain why authorities who held power in the former West Pakistan were reluctant to hold democratic elections.

2. Writing Prompt

Write an article in which you report on the attack by the Pakistani military on Dacca University in March 1971. Begin the article with a strong title that will attract your audience's attention. Include the necessary background to understand the events. Provide details to explain the event and be sure to explain who, what, when, where, and why.

3. Group Activity

In small groups, discuss whether or not India was justified in violating Pakistani territory in order to intervene to stop the crisis in Bangladesh. Have your group write a speech to be presented to the United Nations in which you recommend either that India be censured or commended for its actions.

Overview of the Genocide in East Pakistan

Craig Baxter

Craig Baxter is a former US Foreign Service officer and a retired professor of politics at Juniata College. In the following viewpoint he explains that tensions between West Pakistan and East Pakistan began shortly after Pakistan was separated from India in 1947. Tensions between East and West over parliamentary representation and language differences simmered for decades, Baxter says. Finally, he says, in March 1971, West Pakistan invaded the East, which declared itself the independent state of Bangladesh. As many as three million Bangladeshis may have been killed, wounded, or displaced before India intervened to stop the violence in December, according to Baxter. Bangladesh became a separate nation. He concludes that Bangladesh hoped to prosecute a number of Pakistanis for war crimes, but eventually agreed to drop charges in the interest of peace.

India's independence from Great Britain in August 1947 resulted in the partition of British India into India and Pakistan. Pakistan was created out of the Muslim-majority provinces of

Craig Baxter, *Encyclopedia of Genocide and Crimes Against Humanity*. Belmont, CA: The Gale Group, 2005, pp. 115–119. Copyright © 2005 by The Gale Group. All rights reserved. Reproduced by permission.

British India, with no regard for geographical contiguity. The resulting state was formed into two physically separate wings, with the territory of India intervening between the two. The eastern wing was created by the partition of the British province of Bengal, and the principal language spoken there was Bengali. Although it was principally the language of those who fled India to Pakistan, the government of Pakistan decreed that Urdu would be the national language.

Pakistan Attacks Bangladesh

In the evening of March 25, 1971, the Pakistan army attacked East Pakistan, as the future Bangladesh was then known. The attack was an effort to put down East Pakistani protesters who demanded that the national government recognize the right of the elected majority party, the Awami (People's) League, to assume political office. The attacks by the Pakistanis, and resistance by the Bangladeshis, continued until December of that year, with the Bangladeshis seeing this as a war of independence, and the government forces viewing it as a civil war. Throughout the year, India provided support for the East Pakistani rebels, and received a large number of refugees. Early in December, Pakistan's internal conflict assumed international dimensions with the direct intervention of Indian troops. The violence ended on December 16, when the Pakistani commander at the time, General A. K. Niazi, surrendered to General Jagjeet Singh Aurora, commander of the Indian forces.

History of Discontent

The discontent of East Pakistanis in the united state of Pakistan had a long history before it finally culminated in war. The Muslim League government of Pakistan, led by Muhammad Ali Jinnah, had long ignored East Bengal. However, during his only visit to the eastern province, in March 1948, Jinnah was confronted by Bengalis who demanded that their language be recognized along with Urdu as a co-official language of Pakistan. Jinnah stated that anyone who opposed the status of Urdu as the official language of Pakistan was a traitor to the country. This angered the Bengali faction, and in 1952 that anger gave rise to the "language movement" in East Pakistan.

After independence, the Pakistani government was constituted according to the Government of India Act (1935) as modified by the India Independence Act of 1947, both acts of the British Parliament. It was not until 1956 that a formal constitution was promulgated (India adopted its own constitution in 1950). The constitution of 1956 changed the name of the eastern wing of the country from East Bengal to East Pakistan and the four provinces of the west wing were consolidated into West Pakistan. The constitution also instituted the concept of parity between the eastern and western regions. This meant that representation in the National Assembly would be equal from each province, even though East Pakistan had about 54 percent of the total population of Pakistan. The Bengalis of East Pakistan viewed this as an affront.

This shortchanging of representation in the National Assembly was also seen in the military services. There were very few officers from East Pakistan in a military overwhelmingly dominated by West Pakistanis. There was a similar disparity in representation within the civil service. Although a quota system was later instituted, the disparity persisted at the higher levels throughout the 1960s.

In 1954 a major and violent strike occurred at the Adamjee Jute Mill in Narayanganj, a suburb of Dhaka. In addition to disputes over pay and labor practices, the East Pakistani workers felt that the company was showing favoritism to Urdu-speaking Biharis in employment. *Bihari* is a general term applied to those Urdu-speaking Muslims, most of them from the Indian state of Bihar, who fled east at the time of partition but who never learned to speak Bengali. In addition, the East Pakistani strikers were protesting the fact that the majority of East Pakistan's manufacturing and banking firms were owned by West Pakistanis, among whom the Adamjee family was prominent.

The leading Muslim political party in Bengal prior to Pakistan's independence had been the Muslim League, which dominated the Bengal Provincial Assembly. At the time of independence, the sitting members of the Bengal Provincial Assembly chose their future membership in either the assembly of West Bengal in India or the assembly of East Bengal in Pakistan. The Muslim League maintained control. Although elections were held in each of the provinces of the west wing as early as 1951, elections in East Bengal were delayed until 1954. The election, when it was finally held, resulted in an almost total rout of the Muslim League, which was looked upon locally as a proxy of the central government.

The Awami League

The winning coalition in East Pakistan was comprised of the Awami League and the Krishak Sramik (Farmers and Workers) Party. The principal founder of the Awami League was Husain Shahid Suhrawardy. The Krishak Sramik Party was led by Fazlul Haq. Haq had been a prime minister of united Bengal (i.e., prior to independence) when his party was known as the Krishak Praja (Farmers and Peoples) Party. For the 1954 election, the Awami League and the Krishak Sramik Party joined forces as the United Front and ran for office on a platform called "21 Points." Among the issues addressed by the coalition were the recognition of Bengali as an official language of Pakistan; autonomy for East Bengal in all matters except defense, foreign affairs, and currency; land reform; improved irrigation; nationalization of the jute industry; and other points that, if enacted into law, would give East Bengalis greater control of their own governance.

The demand that Bengali be recognized as an official language was an outgrowth of the language movement of 1952. Since the early days of independence, East Pakistanis had demanded that

Pakistan recognize two official languages: Bengali (the most widely spoken language) and Urdu. An attempt by the central government to devise a means to write Bengali in the Urdu script was met with widespread opposition and rioting, mainly from academics and university students. On February 21, 1952, in an attempt to suppress the violence, the police fired on a crowd of demonstrators, and about twenty students were killed. Today, a monument stands at the site of the killings, and February 21 is celebrated annually as Martyrs' Day.

For its championing of this and other issues important to the majority of East Pakistanis, the Krishak Sramik-Awami League coalition won the 1954 election. Eventually, however, the Krishak Sramik Party withered away, and the Awami League became the most important party in the province. It would become the leader of the independence movement and dominate emerging Bangladeshi politics.

In October 1958 General Muhammad Ayub Khan proclaimed himself president of Pakistan following a military coup, declared martial law, and dissolved the National Assembly and the provincial legislatures. He then set up what he called "Basic Democracy," which he described as a more representative government. Elections at the local level would be direct, and those elected at this level would be designated Basic Democrats. Elections for the provincial and national assemblies and for the presidency would be indirect, with the Basic Democrats serving as the electoral college. He retained the principle of parity, however. This meant that each province was allocated an equal number of Basic Democrat electors, so that East Pakistanis continued to be underrepresented at the higher levels of government. Not unexpectedly, Ayub was elected president in 1962 and reelected president in 1967. Although he won majorities in each wing in each election, his majority in the east wing in 1967 was dramatically less than in 1962.

Nonetheless, Ayub's power began to slip after his reelection to office, as did his health. Opposition to his rule spread, even

Sheik Mujibur Rahman

Sheik Mujibur Rahman (1920–1975) was a charismatic leader who organized dissent and rebellion against the British in India, led the Bengalis of East Pakistan in their resistance to the unjust actions of the post-colonial Pakistani government, and finally helped found the independent nation of Bangladesh in 1972.

Sheik Mujibur Rahman (Mujib) was born on March 17, 1920, in Tongipara village in the Gopalganj subdivision of the Faridpur district in the eastern part of the province of Bengal in British India. An extroverted, sports-loving young man, Mujib was well liked by his teachers and friends, but never distinguished himself in his studies. To the dismay of his father, a small landholder (sheik is one of the titles often assumed by the landed gentry) and a government official, Mujib showed the first sign of his future revolutionary leadership by distributing rice from his father's stockpile to the famine-stricken peasantry of his area.

A charismatic leader, Sheik Mujib epitomized anti-colonial leadership in the Third World. He organized dissent and rebellion against the British and rose against the injustice and exploitation by the power-wielders in West Pakistan against the Bengali population of East Pakistan. For Sheik Mujib the battle for freedom from exploitation was never-ending. Even after winning independence for Bangladesh from Pakistan, an exploitation-free Bengali society eluded him. When he seemed to be having some success in tiding over the most difficult period of post-liberation history, he was assassinated and his family massacred in a fluke coup staged by a handful of junior officers of the fledgling Bangladesh army.

"Mujibur Rahman Sheik," Encyclopedia of World Biography. *Detroit: Gale, 1998.*

in West Pakistan. Ayub grew concerned about a growing secessionist movement in East Pakistan. The Awami League, now headed by Sheik Mujibur Rahman, demanded that changes be made in regard to East Pakistan. These changes were embodied in Mujib's Six Points Plan, which he presented at a meeting of opposition parties in Lahore in 1966. In brief, these Six Points called for:

1. a federal and parliamentary government with free and fair elections;
2. federal government to control only foreign affairs and defense;
3. a separate currency or separate fiscal accounts for each province, to control movement of capital from east to west;
4. all power of taxation to reside at the provincial level, with the federal government subsisting on grants from the provinces;
5. enabling each federating unit to enter into foreign trade agreements on its own and to retain control over the foreign exchange earned; and
6. allowing each unit to raise its own militia.

If these points had been adopted, it would have meant almost de facto independence for East Pakistan. Many observers saw point six, a separate militia, as the point most unacceptable to the central government, but they were wrong. The 1965 Indo-Pakistan War had demonstrated the lack of local defense forces in East Pakistan, which would have left the province defenseless had India attacked there. In fact, it was point four, regarding taxation, that proved to be the problem, because the enactment of this point would make it all but impossible for a central government to operate.

In 1968, in response to the Six Points Plan, the Ayub government charged Mujib and his supporters with treason. This later became known as the Agartala Conspiracy Case, so-called as it was alleged that Mujib had met with Indian agents in Agartala, the capital of the Indian state of Tripura, which borders on Bangladesh. Mujib and the Awami League denied that any such meeting had ever taken place. In early 1969, as hostility to Ayub increased in both East and West Pakistan, he invited opposition leaders to meet with him. Mujib, having been jailed awaiting his trial for treason, was not invited to this meeting. The opposition leaders refused to come to the meeting unless the charges against Mujib were withdrawn and demanded that he, too, be invited to attend. Ayub complied with these demands. The meeting, which Ayub hoped would work to his advantage, instead strengthened the opposition's position, which called for the end of the policy of Basic Democracy and the return to direct parliamentary elections.

General Yahya Khan

The opposition movement expanded beyond the political sphere to the military, and Ayub was forced to resign on March 25, 1969. He was replaced by General Agha Muhammad Yahya Khan, who promised to reinstate direct elections. These were held in December 1970 in most of the country, but flooding in East Pakistan forced a few constituencies to delay their elections until January 1971. In addition to reinstating free and direct elections, Yahya also acted to restore the former provinces of West Pakistan, which had been united into a single unit by the 1956 constitution. More important for East Pakistan, he ended the principle of parity. In the 1970 election for the National Assembly, East Pakistan would have 162 general seats out of a total of 300, reflecting the 54 percent majority that Bengalis enjoyed according to the 1961 population census.

Yahya also introduced legislation that, in his view, would limit the changes that could be made to the constitution by the National Assembly. This legislation, called the Legal Framework Order, touched upon seven points:

1. that Pakistan would be a federated state;
2. Islamic principles would be paramount;
3. direct and regular elections would be held;
4. fundamental rights would be guaranteed;

East Pakistani citizens demonstrate for independence in Dhaka on March 23, 1971, just days before the West Pakistani army attacked the city, killing thousands. © AP Images/Asahi Shimbun.

5. the judiciary would be independent;
6. maximum provincial autonomy would be allowed, "but the federal government shall also have adequate powers, including legislative, administrative, and financial powers, to discharge its responsibilities"; and
7. economic disparities among provinces would be removed.

The result of the election in East Pakistan startled outside observers, and even took some supporters of the Awami League by surprise. The party won 160 of the 162 seats in East Pakistan, thereby gaining a majority in the National Assembly without winning a single seat in West Pakistan, which had thrown its support behind the Pakistan People's Party, led by Zulfikar Ali Bhutto. Neither Yahya, nor his military associates, nor Bhutto looked favorably on a government comprised solely of the Awami League and headed by the author of the Six Points Plan. Yahya began a series of negotiations, perhaps in the hope of creating a coalition government, but more in an effort to sideline Mujib. As the talks became more rancorous and compromise seemed impossible, the Pakistani government began to increase the strength of its rather small contingent of military forces stationed in East Pakistan.

Yahya negotiated with Bhutto and Mujib, the former declaring that there were "two majorities" in Pakistan, and the latter insisting on the full enactment of the Six Points, even where these were at variance with Yahya's Legal Framework Order (i.e., on the issues of taxation). Demonstrations supporting the Awami League's position spread across East Pakistan. Violence began to look more attractive than political activism as a means of protecting East Pakistan's interests. By this time, the term *Bangladeshi* was widely adopted by the Awami League and its supporters to replace the designation *East Pakistani*.

The 1971 War

The army struck back on March 25, 1971. Its first move was to attack the faculty and students at Dhaka University and to take Mujib into custody. By one estimate, up to 35,000 Bangladeshis were killed at the university and elsewhere on the first few days. Mujib was transported to jail in West Pakistan. (There were fears that he would be executed, but these later proved unfounded when he was released at the end of the conflict.) A number of Mujib's associates fled, first to a village on the border with India, then to Calcutta. Major Ziaur Rahman, who would later become president of independent Bangladesh, issued a declaration of independence.

Bangladeshi police and border patrol forces organized a resistance force to oppose the Pakistani army, and they were later joined by several civilians, many of whom had been university students. It was, however, almost nine months before India intervened, triggering the December 16, 1971, surrender of the Pakistani army. India intervened both for strategic reasons (as weakening Pakistan) and for humanitarian reasons, to alleviate the suffering of Bangladeshis.

Pakistan complained about India's invasion of its sovereign territory to the UN Security Council in early December. In an often emotional speech, Bhutto argued, with reason, that this intervention was a violation of international law. The Security Council agreed, but the question soon became moot with the surrender of the Pakistani troops in Bangladesh.

The number of Bangladeshis killed, disabled, raped, or displaced by the violence of 1971 is not fully known. Estimates by Bangladeshi sources put the number killed at up to three million, and it is estimated that as many as ten million may have fled to India. Initially, the Pakistani army targeted educators, students, political leaders, and others who were generally considered to be prominent sympathizers of the Awami League. As the Bangladeshis formed military units, however, these units also became the targets. Some of these units were formed by Bangladeshis who had formerly served in the Pakistani army; others were recruited from the police and the East Pakistan (now Bangladesh) Rifles, a border security force. These units, based in rural and outlying areas of Bangladesh, were able to take advantage of the Pakistani army's initial focus on the student-led demonstrations in the Dhaka region. Survivor accounts, such as that by Jahanara Imam, suggest that much of the killing soon devolved into little more than indiscriminate slaughter.

The Pakistani surrender and the termination of conflict left several unsettled questions. Many Bangladeshis—mostly civil servants or military troops and their families—were still detained in Pakistan. In Bangladesh, there were non-Bengalis—

again, mostly civil servants or military troops, but also some business owners and professionals—who wished repatriation to Pakistan. In addition, the fate of de facto prisoners of war held by Bangladesh, and Pakistani prisoners of war held by India had yet to be decided. Bangladesh wanted to place 195 Pakistani military personnel on trial for war crimes and genocide. On August 9, 1975, a tripartite agreement between Bangladesh, India, and Pakistan was reached to create a panel that would attempt to settle these issues. Bangladesh also agreed to drop all charges against the 195 Pakistanis accused of war crimes and to permit their repatriation to Pakistan.

In the end, and at great cost, Bangladesh achieved its independence. Slowly, the two countries were able to establish diplomatic relations. Pakistan recognized Bangladesh as independent on February 22, 1974, primarily at the urging of the Organization of the Islamic Conference (OIC), which was meeting in Lahore at that time. The OIC insisted that Bangladesh, a Muslim state, be permitted to attend the conference. Bangladeshis, however, remained unsatisfied. They wanted an apology from the Pakistanis for the excesses committed during the war. They received one finally from the Pakistani president, Pervez Musharraf, when he visited Bangladesh in July 2002.

Bangladesh Proclaims Independence

Bangladesh Proclamation of Independence

The Bangladeshi government in exile proclaims Bangladesh's independence from Pakistan in 1971. The document states that Pakistan illegally ignored and sidelined Bangladesh's official representatives to the legislature. It also says that Pakistan declared an unjust war upon Bangladesh and committed numerous atrocities and genocide against the Bangladeshi people. The document says, therefore, that Bangladesh is independent from Pakistan and declares Sheikh Mujibur Rahman as the president of Bangladesh. The document also states that the declaration of independence came into effect March 10 and says that Bangladesh will draw up a constitution.

Mujibnagar, Bangladesh
Dated 10th day of April, 1971.

Whereas free elections were held in Bangladesh from 7th December, 1970 to 17th January, 1971, to elect representatives for the purpose of framing a Constitution,

AND

Whereas at these elections the people of Bangladesh elected 167 out of 169 representatives belonging to the Awami League [a political group that led the movement for greater autonomy for Bangladesh],

AND

Whereas General Yahya Khan [the leader of Pakistan] summoned the elected representatives of the people to meet on the 3rd March, 1971, for the purpose of framing a Constitution,

AND

Whereas the Assembly so summoned was arbitrarily and illegally postponed for indefinite period,

AND

Whereas instead of fulfilling their promise and while still conferring with the representatives of the people of Bangladesh, Pakistan authorities declared an unjust and treacherous war,

AND

Whereas in the facts and circumstances of such treacherous conduct Bangabandhu Sheikh Mujibur Rahman, the undisputed leader of the 75 million people of Bangladesh, in due fulfillment of the legitimate right of self-determination of the people of Bangladesh, duly made a declaration of independence at Dacca on March 26, 1971, and urged the people of Bangladesh to defend the honour and integrity of Bangladesh,

AND

Whereas in the conduct of a ruthless and savage war the Pakistani authorities committed and are still continuously committing numerous acts of genocide and unprecedented tortures, amongst others on the civilian and unarmed people of Bangladesh,

AND

Whereas the Pakistan Government by levying an unjust war and committing genocide and by other repressive measures made it impossible for the elected representatives of the people of Bangladesh to meet and frame a Constitution, and give to themselves a Government,

AND

Whereas the people of Bangladesh by their heroism, bravery and revolutionary fervour have established effective control over the territories of Bangladesh, We the elected representatives of the people of Bangladesh, as honour bound by the mandate given to us by the people of Bangladesh whose will is supreme duly constituted ourselves into a Constituent Assembly, and

having held mutual consultations, and

in order to ensure for the people of Bangladesh equality, human dignity and social justice,

declare and constitute Bangladesh to be sovereign Peoples' Republic and thereby confirm the declaration of independence already made by Bangabandhu Sheikh Mujibur Rahman, and

do hereby affirm and resolve that till such time as a Constitution is framed, Bangabandhu Sheikh Mujibur Rahman shall be the President of the Republic and that Syed Nazrul Islam shall be the Vice President of the Republic, and

that the President shall be the Supreme Commander of all the Armed Forces of the Republic,

shall exercise all the Executive and Legislative powers of the Republic including the power to grant pardon,

shall have the power to appoint a Prime Minister and such other Ministers as he considers necessary,

shall have the power to levy taxes and expend monies,

shall have the power to summon and adjourn the Constituent Assembly, and

do all other things that may be necessary to give to the people of Bangladesh an orderly and just Government,

We the elected representatives of the people of Bangladesh do further resolve that in the event of there being no President or the President being unable to enter upon his office or being unable to exercise his powers and duties, due to any reason whatsoever, the Vice-President shall have and exercise all the powers, duties and responsibilities herein conferred on the President,

Sheikh Mujibur Rahman, seen speaking in front of the flag symbolizing Bangladeshi liberation, was named acting president in the Proclamation of Independence as of March 10, 1971. He was jailed soon thereafter by West Pakistan. © AP Images.

We further resolve that we undertake to observe and give effect to all duties and obligations that devolve upon us as a member of the family of nations and under the Charter of United Nations,

We further resolve that this proclamation of independence shall be deemed to have come into effect from 26th day of March, 1971.

We further resolve that in order to give effect to this instrument we appoint Prof. Yusuf Ali our duly Constituted Potentiary and to give to the President and the Vice-President oaths of office.

India Supported Bangladesh and Went to War Against Pakistan

Owen Bennett Jones

Owen Bennett Jones is a journalist for BBC Online. In the follow-ing viewpoint, he says that India intervened in the civil war on the side of Bangladesh, both for strategic reasons and to stem the flow of refugees. Jones argues that India's superior airpower and the support it received from Mukti Bahini fighters on the ground gave it a massive advantage over Pakistan. He says that Pakistan also made diplomatic errors and failed to isolate India internationally for its illegal violation of Pakistan's borders. Though Pakistani gen-erals have been blamed for the loss, Jones concludes that Pakistan had little chance of victory once India entered the war.

It is not clear exactly when the Indian prime minister Indira Gandhi decided to go to war. Initially, Delhi [the Indian capital] believed that Operation Searchlight [the West Pakistani attack on Bangladesh] would be a short-lived affair, followed by a negotiated settlement in which the East Pakistanis would accept the unity of the country. But as the Pakistani army's campaign continued, and refugees flowed into India, opinion in Delhi hardened. By June

Pakistani general A.K. Niazi (seated right) officially surrendered to Indian general Jagjit Singh Aurora (seated left) on December 16, 1971. Once India made the decision to enter the conflict, Pakistan was quickly defeated. © Bettmann/Corbis.

[1971], there was an emerging consensus that an independent Bangladesh was in India's interests and might even be worth fighting for. In July 1971, Lt. General Jagjit Singh Aurora was given the job of destroying the Pakistani forces in East Pakistan. He was also given half a million men to complete the task.

International War

The first Indian attacks were limited to strikes on Pakistani forces followed by rapid withdrawals back to Indian territory.

By 21 November, though, the Indians started digging in on East Pakistani soil. From the point of view of the military tacticians in Delhi, the timing could not have been better. The end of the monsoon meant that they would not be held up by torrential rain while the arrival of snow in the passes on the Chinese-Indian border limited Beijing's [that is, China's] military options should it want to get involved.

[Pakistan President] Yahya [Khan] responded to the Indian incursions by opening up the western front. He launched air attacks on nine airbases in north-west India on 3 December. The attacks were futile: due to faulty intelligence, not one Indian aircraft was destroyed. Yahya then ordered some limited ground offensives intended to draw the Indian forces in the west into the open. Throughout the war, though, Yahya never launched a full-blown offensive on the western front. That is not to say there wasn't some fierce fighting on the borders of West Pakistan: there was. The two armies clashed in Kashmir and in Sindh but these engagements were never on a big enough scale to affect the outcome of the war as a whole. On the many occasions when Yahya was urged to act more decisively in the west and commit more troops there, he always expressed reluctance to do so. Maybe he was afraid of defeat. For all the theorising, the defence of East Pakistan was to lie in the east.

After the Pakistani air strikes, Delhi could claim that Pakistan had dealt the first blow and India's full-scale invasion of the east, originally scheduled for 6 December, was brought forward. The Indian air force inflicted the first major damage by hitting Dhaka's military airport. Pakistan's squadron of Sabre fighter-jets were unable to take off and could play no part in the war: India enjoyed complete air superiority. It also had a significant manpower advantage, although its extent has been vigorously disputed. At one extreme Lt. General [Amir Abdullah Khan] Niazi has claimed that, at most, he had 55,000 men under his command and that 'the ratio of troops between us and the Indians came to approximately one to ten'. The Hamoodur

Rehman Commission [constituted by Pakistan to investigate Pakistan's defeat during the war] report challenged these figures and estimated the Pakistani forces at between 73,000 and 93,000, while the Indians have suggested a one to eight ratio. The numbers are complicated by the fact that the Indians could rely on the highly motivated [Bangladeshi resistance fighters the] Mukti Bahini (generally estimated at 100,000) whilst Niazi had far less effective support from various irregular forces, including some 'Mujahid Battalions' and madrasa students. India also had a clear advantage in terms of military equipment. Indeed, the Pakistanis were short of many basic items such as land-mines. In some places, they had to create lines of defence with nothing more than sharpened bamboo sticks stuck in the ground.

Inevitable Defeat

Lt. General Niazi never stood a chance. When the Hamoodur Rehman Commission questioned Yahya Khan and other senior generals, they freely conceded that, once India launched a full-scale invasion, defeat was inevitable. Niazi was outnumbered, outgunned and operating in territory with a hostile population. Despite his hopeless situation, many Pakistanis have been strongly critical of his strategy in East Pakistan and have blamed him for the army's humiliation. The arguments about his record mainly concern his defensive strategy. Niazi repeatedly claimed that he would defend Dhaka to the 'last man, last bullet'. But rather than concentrate his forces there he spread them all along East Pakistan's 2,500-mile land border in small groups to hold up any Indian attack. Niazi said there was to be no withdrawal from these positions until 75 per cent casualties had been taken. One military historian described this as the most stupid order given during the whole war. . . .

Pakistani writers have generally used a different argument to criticise Niazi. In line with the findings of the Hamoodur Rehman Commission, they say that Niazi should have concentrated his forces in Dhaka. The capital of East Pakistan, they argue, was always India's ultimate objective and the fact that it was surrounded by rivers on three sides rendered it highly defensible. Had Niazi concentrated his forces there, the argument goes, he would have been able to hold up the Indians for longer. This reasoning is, however, unconvincing. The Indians would have been able to move through East Pakistan at will before besieging Dhaka. With a hostile population, and Indian air superiority, it is difficult to see how Niazi could have successfully defended the city. Furthermore, many of those who have criticised the fortress concept would have been the first to blame Niazi if he had let the Indians move through East Pakistan unopposed. . . .

Niazi was asked to hold out as long as possible so that Yahya had time to rustle up some international support. Pakistan's plan had been turned on its head. The defence of the west now lay in the east. With Pakistan's strategists in disarray, Indira Gandhi, on 6 December, told the Indian parliament that her government recognised Bangladesh as an independent and sovereign state. She was confident of victory. General Niazi, meanwhile, seemed sure of defeat. He sent the following message to GHQ [General Headquarters] in Rawalpindi:

> . . . Indian air force causing maximum damage(.) have started using rockets and napalm against own defensive positions(.) internally rebels highly active, emboldened and causing maximum damage in all possible ways including cutting of means of communication(.) this including destruction of roads/ bridges/rail/ferries/boats etc.(.) local populations also against us(.) lack of communications making it difficult to reinforce or replenish or readjust positions . . . resorting to fortress/ strong point basis(.) enemy will be involved though all methods including unorthodox action will fight it out to last man last round(.) request expedite actions vide your G-0235 of 5 Dec 1971

Niazi was alarmed because the Indians were moving through East Pakistan with extraordinary speed. Rather than engage the fortresses one by one, they simply bypassed them. The fact that they were working closely with the Mukti Bahini, who knew the territory of East Pakistan well, helped the Indian forces find routes that the Pakistanis had not anticipated. . . .

Diplomatic Failure

Pakistan's hopeless military situation on the ground was matched on the diplomatic front. The Indians' diplomatic position would have been far worse if Yahya had acted with greater speed and determination to isolate Delhi for what was, after all, a blatantly illegal invasion of a foreign country. Amazingly, Yahya failed to raise the Indian invasion of Pakistan formally at the UN Security Council. He probably feared that any ceasefire resolution would include a provision that he had to negotiate with the Awami League [the political party favoring Bangladesh's independence]—something he was determined to avoid. But whatever the rationale, it was a significant blunder.

The Security Council did nevertheless discuss the situation in East Pakistan but successive resolutions were vetoed by either Russia or China. The Russians, backing India, wanted any resolution to include commitments for a transfer of power to the Awami League; the Chinese, backing Pakistan, did not. In his capacity of foreign minister [for Pakistan], Zulfikar Ali Bhutto went to New York but was unable to affect the course of events. With Pakistan's unity on the verge of destruction and frustrated by the Russians' Security Council vetoes, Bhutto decided to make the best of a bad job and strengthen his own political position back at home. On 15 December he told the Security Council that he would never address them again. As he ripped up some Security Council papers, he asked: 'Why should I waste my time here? I will go back to my country and fight.' It was the speech of a leader in waiting.

Despite the bleak communications emanating from Dhaka, Niazi has claimed that when the war came to a close Pakistan's position was not so bad:

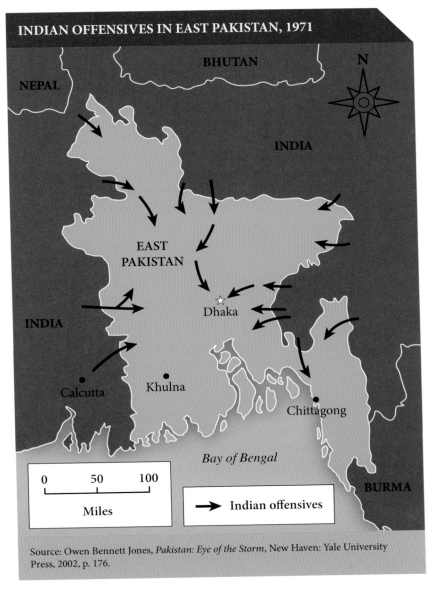

INDIAN OFFENSIVES IN EAST PAKISTAN, 1971

BHUTAN

N

NEPAL

INDIA

EAST
PAKISTAN

Dhaka

INDIA

Calcutta

Khulna

Chittagong

Bay of Bengal

0   50   100

Miles

→ Indian offensives

BURMA

Source: Owen Bennett Jones, *Pakistan: Eye of the Storm*, New Haven: Yale University Press, 2002, p. 176.

In fact when the time for an attack against Dhaka came, they [the Indians] were left with only four weak brigades. All the rest were fighting isolated battles against us and our well-stocked and well-prepared fortresses, and were having a tough time with heavy casualties. Aurora could not move his troops from these sectors to concentrate against Dhaka, his ultimate objective.

Indian accounts of the war confirm many of Niazi's claims. General Jacob has described how he found himself in an increasingly awkward position. The Indian army chief, General Sam Manekshaw, had always made it clear that he did not consider Dhaka to be the primary objective for the Indian invaders. He argued that if the Indian forces took Chittagong and Khulna then Dhaka would automatically fall. His officers on the ground, however, wanted the big prize and struck straight for Dhaka. As international pressure for a ceasefire built up Manekshaw became ever more concerned that this focus on Dhaka was going to have disastrous consequences. He could foresee a ceasefire being imposed before India had taken any of East Pakistan's major towns.

'On 13 December', recalls General Jacob, 'we received a signal from Gen Manekshaw ordering us to immediately capture all the towns in Bangladesh that we had bypassed. All the towns were named with the exception of Dacca. These included Dinajpur, Rangpur, Sylhet, Maynamati Cantonment and also Khulna and Chittagong.' Jacob was dismayed:

> We had reached the outskirts of Dacca and to me it was imperative that we capture Dacca rather than waste our efforts in going back and capturing those towns. Had we done so, our operations would have been bogged down. The only towns which we had been able to occupy were Jessore and Comilla from which the Pakistanis had withdrawn.

General Jacob needed Pakistan to surrender as quickly as possible and he opted for some psychological warfare. He was greatly helped by the success of Indian intelligence operatives in intercepting messages between Dhaka and Rawalpindi, which indicated that morale in Dhaka was desperately low. Jacob then received another useful piece of intelligence: he was told that the East Pakistani governor had called a high-powered meeting in Government House on 14 December. Having looked up the location of the building on a tourist map Jacob ordered an air strike on it.

It was a masterful tactic. Niazi's public relations officer, Siddiq Salik, was at the receiving end and described what happened. The Indian bombs, he recalled,

> ripped the massive roof of the main hall. The Governor rushed to the air raid shelter and scribbled out his resignation. Almost all the inmates of this seat of power survived the raid. Except for some fish in a decorative glass case. They restlessly tossed on the hot rubble and breathed their last.

Surrender

Jacob's air raid had finished off not only the fish but also the West Pakistanis' will. The governor, his cabinet and some West Pakistani civil servants headed to the safety of the Hotel Intercontinental. The Red Cross, which had declared the hotel to be a neutral zone, refused to let them in unless they disassociated themselves from the Pakistani government. The terrified governor and his colleagues readily agreed.

On 14 December President Yahya sent Niazi this message:

> you have fought a heroic battle against overwhelming odds(.) the nation is proud of you and the world full of admiration(.) I have done all that is humanly possible to find an acceptable solution to the problem(.) you have now reached a stage when further resistance is no longer humanly possible nor will it serve any useful purpose(.) you should now take all necessary measures to stop the fighting and preserve the lives of all armed forces personnel from West Pakistan . . .

That evening Niazi went to see Herbert Spivack, the US consul general in Dhaka, to send a message to the Indian army chief requesting a ceasefire. By 16 December negotiations were sufficiently advanced for General Jacob to go to Dhaka. It was a difficult assignment. Niazi was still hoping to sign a ceasefire document and not a surrender. As Jacob recalled: 'Colonel Khara read out the terms of surrender. There was dead silence in the room as tears streamed down Niazi's cheeks . . . I asked him whether the document was acceptable. He handed it back without comment. I took this as acceptance.' To Niazi's dismay, Jacob then made it clear that his surrender would be in public.

The United States Tilted Toward Pakistan During the War

Claude Arpi

Claude Arpi is a French-born author, journalist, historian, and Tibetologist. In the following viewpoint he argues that US president Richard Nixon and secretary of state Henry Kissinger favored West Pakistan during the 1971 war. Arpi says that Nixon and Kissinger were primarily interested in forming closer relations with China, which supported Pakistan, and with thwarting the Soviet Union, which opposed Pakistan. Arpi says that Nixon and Kissinger ignored warnings by diplomats in Bangladesh that the United States was allowing a humanitarian disaster. Arpi concludes that Nixon and Kissinger were upset at India's decision to go to war, but were ultimately pleased that West Pakistan remained unified, even though Bangladesh gained its independence.

A few months ago [2006], the Office of the Historian at the US State Department released Volume XI of the Foreign Relations of the United States devoted to the 'South Asia Crisis, 1971': in other words, the Bangladesh War.

Flashback: 1971 War, Thirty-Five Years On

This 929-page publication groups together documents which were already known like the minutes of Henry Kissinger's secret visit to China in July 1971 as well as scores of freshly declassified material available for the first time to the public.

It throws light on a less known angle of the India-Pakistan conflict: The role of the nascent friendship between the United States and China. This is a welcome new piece in the puzzle of the history of the 1971 War.

Another piece is the Hamidur Rahman Report, ordered by the government of Pakistan after the war, which analyses the Pakistani defeat. 'Due to corruption... lust for wine and women and greed for land and houses, a large number of senior army officers, particularly those occupying the highest positions, had not only lost the will to fight but also the professional competence necessary for taking the vital and critical decisions demanded of them for the successful prosecution of the war.'

The US Administration Saw the Events Differently

According to Kissinger, then American President Richard M Nixon's national security adviser, 'When the Nixon administration took office, our policy objective on the subcontinent was, quite simply, to avoid adding another complication to our agenda.'

But events in the subcontinent and the Chinese factor forced Nixon to change his stand. The new closeness between Washington, DC and Beijing and the involvement of the Pakistan president as a secret go-between greatly influenced US policy.

According to the State Department historian, 'When the fighting developed, the Nixon administration tilted toward Pakistan. The tilt involved the dispatch of the aircraft carrier *USS Enterprise* to the Bay of Bengal to try to intimidate the Indian government. It also involved encouraging China to make military moves to achieve the same end, and an assurance to China that if China menaced India and the Soviet Union moved against

US president Richard Nixon (right) meets with Pakistan president Agha Yahya Khan at the White House in 1970, only months before East and West Pakistan began their civil war. © Bettmann/Corbis.

China in support of India, the United States would protect China from the Soviet Union. China chose not to menace India, and the crisis on the subcontinent ended without a confrontation between the United States and the Soviet Union.'

The first US documents deal with the background of the conflict. Nixon's position was clear: 'We should just stay out—like in Biafra [a secessionist state that attempted to gain independence from Nigeria], what the hell can we do?'

But everybody did not agree with him. In a telegram sent on March 28, 1971, the staff at the US consulate in Dhaka [Bangladesh] complained, 'Our government has failed to denounce the suppression of democracy. Our government has failed to denounce atrocities. Our government has failed to take forceful measures to protect its citizens while at the same time bending over backwards to placate the West Pak dominated government. . . . We, as professional public servants express our dissent with current policy and fervently hope that our true and lasting interests here can be defined and our policies redirected in order to salvage our nation's position as a moral leader of the free world.'

When US Secretary of State Will Rogers received this 'miserable' cable, he informed President Nixon that the 'Dacca consulate is in open rebellion.' This did not change Nixon's opinion: 'The people who bitch about Vietnam bitch about it because we intervened in what they say is a civil war. Now some of the same bastards . . . want us to intervene here—both civil wars.'

From the start, the Nixon administration knew 'the prospects were "poor" . . . the Pakistani army would not be able to exert effective control over East Pakistan.' Washington believed India was bound to support Mujibur Rahman. The CIA had reported that 'India would foster and support Bengali insurgency and contribute to the likelihood that an independent Bangladesh would emerge from the developing conflict.'

The Chinese Saga

It is here that the Chinese saga began. In a tightly guarded secret, Nixon had started contacts with Beijing. The postman was Pakistani dictator Field Marshal Yahya Khan.

When on April 28, 1971, Kissinger sent a note defining the future policy option towards Pakistan, Nixon replied in a handwritten note: 'Don't squeeze Yahya [Khan, the Pakistan president] at this time.' The Pakistan president was not to be squeezed because he was in the process of arranging Kissinger's first secret meeting to China. The events of the following months and the US position should be seen in this perspective.

In May, Indira Gandhi wrote to Nixon about the 'carnage in East Bengal' and the flood of refugees burdening India. After L K Jha, then the Indian ambassador to US, had warned Kissinger that India might have to send back some of the refugees as guerillas, Nixon commented, 'By God we will cut off economic aid (*to India*).'

A few days later when the US president said 'the goddamn Indians' were preparing for another war, Kissinger retorted 'they are the most aggressive goddamn people around.'

During the second week of July [1971], Kissinger went to Beijing where he was told by then Chinese prime minister Zhou Enlai: 'In our opinion, if India continues on its present course in disregard of world opinion, it will continue to go on recklessly. We, however, support the stand of Pakistan. This is known to the world. If they (*the Indians*) are bent on provoking such a situation, then we cannot sit idly by.' Kissinger answered that Zhou should know that the US sympathies also lay with Pakistan.

On his return, during a meeting of the National Security Council, Nixon continued his India bashing. The Indians, he noted, are 'a slippery, treacherous people.'

The State Department historian says, 'in the perspective of Washington, the crisis ratcheted up a dangerous notch on August 9 when India and the Soviet Union signed a treaty of peace, friendship and cooperation.' It was a shock for Washington as they saw a deliberate collusion between Delhi [India] and Moscow [Russia].

During the following months, the situation deteriorated and many more refugees came to India. The Indian prime minister decided to tour Western capitals to explain the Indian stand. On November 4 and 5, she met Nixon in Washington, who told her that a new war in the subcontinent was out of the question.

The next day, Nixon and Kissinger assessed the situation. Kissinger told Nixon: 'The Indians are bastards anyway. They are plotting a war.'

The War Begins

To divert the pressure applied by the Mukti Bahini [the Bangladeshi independence fighters] on the eastern front, the Pakistan air force launched an attack on six Indian airfields in Kashmir and Punjab on December 3. It was the beginning of the war.

The next day, then US ambassador to the United Nations George H W Bush—later 41st president of the United States and father of the [43rd] American president [George W. Bush]—introduced a resolution in the UN Security Council calling for a cease-fire and the withdrawal of armed forces by India and Pakistan. It was vetoed by the Soviet Union. The following days witnessed a great pressure on the Soviets from the Nixon-Kissinger duo to get India to withdraw, but to no avail.

The CIA reported to the President: 'She (*Indira Gandhi*) hopes the Chinese (*will*) not intervene physically in the North; however, the Soviets have warned her that the Chinese are still able to "rattle the sword" in Ladakh and Chumbi areas.'

For Kissinger it was clear that Indira Gandhi wanted the dis-memberment of Pakistan.

On December 9, when the CIA director warned Nixon that 'East Pakistan was crumbling', Nixon decided to send the aircraft carrier *USS Enterprise* into the Bay of Bengal to threaten India.

Let me recount an anecdote related to me by Major General K K Tewari (retd), Chief Signal Officer, Eastern Command, during the 1971 War.

General Tewari was present at a briefing the three defence services held for Indira Gandhi. She was seated at a large table. On one side was General S H F J Manekshaw, the army chief, and on the other Admiral S M Nanda, the navy chief.

During the course of the presentation, the admiral intervened and said: 'Madam, the US 8th Fleet is sailing into the Bay of Bengal.' Nothing happened; the briefing continued. After some time, the admiral repeated, 'Madam, I have to inform you that the 8th Fleet is sailing into the Bay of Bengal.' She cut him off immediately: 'Admiral, I heard you the first time, let us go on with the briefing.'

All the officers present were stunned. Ultimately, their morale was tremendously boosted by the prime minister's attitude. She had demonstrated her utter contempt for the American bluff.

On November 10, Nixon instructed Kissinger to ask the Chinese to move some troops toward the Indian frontier. 'Threaten to move forces or move them, Henry, that's what they must do now.'

This was conveyed to Huang Hua, China's envoy to the United Nations. Kissinger told Huang the US would be prepared for a military confrontation with the Soviet Union if the Soviet Union attacked China.

On December 12, the White House received an urgent message. The Chinese wanted to meet in New York. General Alexander Haig, then Kissinger's deputy, rushed to the venue, but was disappointed. Huang just wanted to convey his government's stand in the UN, no words of an attack in Sikkim or in the then North East Frontier Agency (now, the northeastern states). . . .

Until the last day of the war, Pakistan expected its Chinese saviour to strike, but Beijing never did.

In Washington, Nixon analysed the situation thus: 'If the Russians get away with facing down the Chinese and the Indians get away with licking the Pakistanis . . . we may be looking down the gun barrel.' Nixon was not sure about China. Did they really intend to start a military action against India?

Finally, on December 16, [General Amir Abdullah Khan] Niazi surrendered to Lieutenant General Jagjit Singh Aurora. Nixon and Kissinger congratulated themselves for achieving their fundamental goal—the preservation of West Pakistan. They were also happy for having 'scared the pants off the Russians.'

Kissinger's South Asia policy upset many in the US, not only the American public, the press but also the State Department, and more particularly, Secretary of State Rogers who was kept in the dark most of the time.

India, Pakistan, and Bangladesh Agree to Return to Peace

Tripartite Agreement Between India, Bangladesh and Pakistan for Normalisation of Relations in the Subcontinent

The Tripartite Agreement between India, Bangladesh, and Pakistan was a treaty ending the conflict between the three nations. The agreement declares that all three countries are committed to good relations in the region, and that they wish to resume normal relations following the 1971 war. Specifically, the agreement consents to repatriate Pakistanis in Bangladesh, Bangladeshis in Pakistan, and Pakistani prisoners of war in India to their home countries. The agreement also states that Bangladesh will not try 195 captured Pakistanis for war crimes. Instead, Bangladesh agrees in the interest of peace to forgive and forget and to allow the accused Pakistanis to return home to Pakistan.

New Delhi, April 9, 1974.

1. On July 2, 1972, the President of Pakistan and the Prime Minister of India signed an historic agreement at Shimla [India] under which they resolved that the two countries put an end to the conflict and confrontation that have hitherto marred their relations and work for the promotion of a friendly and

"Tripartite Agreement Between India, Bangladesh and Pakistan for Normalisation of Relations in the Subcontinent," Stateless People in Bangladesh, www.statelesspeopleinban gladesh.net, April 9, 1974. Courtesy of Stateless People in Bangladesh. All rights reserved. Reproduced by permission.

harmonious relationship and the establishment of durable peace in the sub-continent. The Agreement also provided for the settlement of "their differences by peaceful means through bilateral negotiations or by any other peaceful means mutually agreed upon."

Peace in the Region

2. Bangladesh welcomed the Shimla Agreement. The Prime Minister of Bangladesh strongly supported its objective of reconciliation, good neighborliness and establishment of durable peace in the sub-continent [the region of India, Pakistan, and Bangladesh].

3. The humanitarian problems arising in the wake of the tragic events of 1971 constituted a major obstacle in the way of reconciliation and normalisation among the countries of the sub-continent. In the absence of recognition, it was not possible to have tripartite talks to settle the humanitarian problems, as Bangladesh could not participate in such a meeting except on the basis of sovereign equality.

4. On April 17, 1973 India and Bangladesh took a major step forward to break the deadlock on the humanitarian issues by setting aside the political problems of recognition. In a Declaration issued on that date they said that they "are resolved to continue their efforts to reduce tension, promote friendly and harmonious relationship in the sub-continent and work together towards the establishment of a durable peace." Inspired by this vision and "in the larger interests of reconciliation, peace and stability in the sub-continent" they jointly proposed that the problem of the detained and stranded persons should be resolved on humanitarian considerations through simultaneous repatriation of all such persons except those Pakistani prisoners of war who might be required by the Government of Bangladesh for trial on certain charges.

5. Following the Declaration there were a series of talks between India and Bangladesh and India and Pakistan. These

talks resulted in an agreement at Delhi on August 28, 1973 between India and Pakistan with the concurrence of Bangladesh, which provided for a solution on the outstanding humanitarian problems.

6. In pursuance of this Agreement, the process of three-way repatriation commenced on September 19, 1973. So far nearly 300,000 persons have been repatriated which has generated an atmosphere of reconciliation and paved the way for normalisation of relations in the sub-continent.

Recognition and Repatriation

7. In February 1974, recognition took place thus facilitating the participation of Bangladesh in the tripartite meeting envisaged in the Delhi Agreement, on the basis of sovereign equality. Accordingly His Excellency Dr. Kamal Hossain, Foreign Minister of the Government of Bangladesh, His Excellency Sardar Swaran Singh, Minister of External Affairs, Government of India and His Excellency Mr. Aziz Ahmed, Minister of State for Defense and Foreign Affairs of the Government of Pakistan met in New Delhi from April 5th to April 9th, 1974 and discussed the various issues mentioned in the Delhi Agreement in particular the question of the 195 prisoners of war and the completion of the three-way process of repatriation involving Bengalese in Pakistan, Pakistanis in Bangladesh and Pakistani prisoners of war in India.

8. The Ministers reviewed the progress of the three-way repatriation under the Delhi Agreement of August 28, 1973. They were gratified that such a large number of persons detained or stranded in the three countries had since reached their destinations.

9. The Ministers also considered steps that needed to be taken in order expeditiously to bring the process of the three-way repatriation to a satisfactory conclusion.

10. The Indian side stated that the remaining Pakistani prisoners of war and civilian internees in India to be repatriated

Pakistani president Zulfikar Ali Bhutto (left) shakes hands with Indian prime minister Indira Gandhi after signing a peace agreement in Shimla, India, 1972. The agreement marked the end of Indian intervention in the civil war that divided Pakistan and Bangladesh. © AP Images.

under the Delhi Agreement, numbering approximately 6,500, would be repatriated at the usual pace of a train on alternate days and the likely short-fall due to the suspension of trains from April 10th to April 19th, 1974 on account of Kumbh Mela, would be made up by running additional trains after April 19th. It was thus hoped that the repatriation of prisoners of war would be completed by the end of April 1974.

11. The Pakistan side stated that the repatriation of Bangladesh nationals from Pakistan was approaching completion. The remaining Bangladesh nationals in Pakistan would also be repatriated without let or hindrance.

12. In respect of non-Bengalese in Bangladesh, the Pakistan side stated that the Government of Pakistan had already issued clearances for movement to Pakistan in favour of those non-Bengalees who were either domiciled in former West Pakistan, were employees of the Central Government and their families or were members of the divided families, irrespective of their original domicile. The issuance of clearances to 25,000 persons who constitute hardship cases was also in progress. The Pakistan side reiterated that all those who fall under the first three categories would be received by Pakistan without any limit as to numbers. In respect of persons whose applications had been rejected, the Government of Pakistan would, upon request, provide reasons why any particular case was rejected. Any aggrieved applicant could, at any time, seek a review of his application provided he was able to supply new facts or further information to the Government of Pakistan in support of his contention that he qualified in one or other of the three categories. The claims of such persons would not be time-barred. In the event of the decision of review of a case being adverse, the Governments of Pakistan and Bangladesh might seek to resolve it by mutual consultation.

Forgive and Forget

13. The question of 195 Pakistani prisoners of war was discussed by the three Ministers, in the context of the earnest desire of the Governments for reconciliation, peace and friendship in the sub-continent. The Foreign Minister of Bangladesh stated that the excesses and manifold crimes committed by these prisoners of war constituted, according to the relevant provisions of the U.N. General Assembly Resolutions and International Law, war

crimes, crimes against humanity and genocide, and that there was universal consensus that persons charged with such crimes as the 195 Pakistani prisoners of war should be held to account and subjected to the due process of law. The Minister of State for Defense and Foreign Affairs of the Government of Pakistan said that his Government condemned and deeply regretted any crimes that may have been committed.

14. In this connection the three Ministers noted that the matter should be viewed in the context of the determination of the three countries to continue resolutely to work for reconciliation. The Ministers further noted that following recognition; the Prime Minister of Pakistan had declared that he would visit Bangladesh in response to the invitation of the Prime Minister of Bangladesh and appeal to the people of Bangladesh to forgive and forget the mistakes of the past in order to promote reconciliation. Similarly, the Prime Minister of Bangladesh had declared with regard to the atrocities and destruction committed in Bangladesh in 1971 that he wanted the people to forget the past and to make a fresh start, stating that the people of Bangladesh knew how to forgive.

15. In the light of the foregoing and, in particular, having regard to the appeal of the Prime Minister of Pakistan to the people of Bangladesh to forgive and forget the mistakes of the past, the Foreign Minister of Bangladesh stated that the Government of Bangladesh had decided not to proceed with the trials as an act of clemency. It was agreed that the 195 prisoners of war may be repatriated to Pakistan along with the other prisoners of war now in the process of repatriation under the Delhi Agreement.

16. The Ministers expressed their conviction that the above agreements provide a firm basis for the resolution of the humanitarian problems arising out of the conflict of 1971. They reaffirmed the vital stake the seven hundred million people of the three countries have in peace and progress and reiterated the resolve of their Governments to work for the promotion of nor-

malisation of relations and the establishment of durable peace in the sub-continent.

Signed in New Delhi on April 9th, 1974 in three originals, each of which is equally authentic.

Kamal Hossain	Swaran Singh	Aziz Ahmed
[Minister of Foreign Affairs, Bangladesh]	[External Affairs Minister, India]	[Minister of State for Defense and Foreign Affairs, Pakistan]

CHAPTER 2

Controversies Surrounding the East Pakistan Genocide

Chapter Exercises

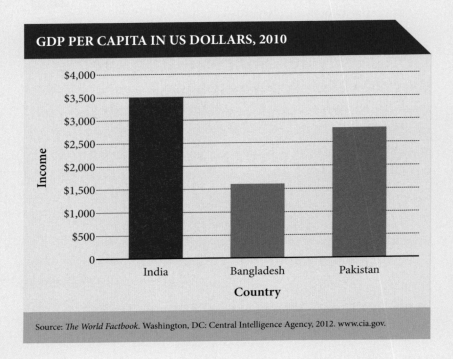

GDP PER CAPITA IN US DOLLARS, 2010

Source: *The World Factbook*. Washington, DC: Central Intelligence Agency, 2012. www.cia.gov.

1. Analyze the Graph

Question 1: GDP per capita is a measure of a country's total income per person; that is, it is basically average yearly income. In which of the countries here are the people on average least well off?

Question 2: What is the approximate difference in per capita GDP between Bangladesh and Pakistan?

Question 3: China's per capita GDP (not shown) was $7,600 in 2010. This is about twice the per capita GDP of which country on the graph?

2. Writing Prompt

Imagine you are a blogger for an international nonprofit covering war crimes issues. Write a post in which you explain why the war crimes tribunal in Bangladesh is or is not advancing the cause of justice.

3. Group Activity

Form groups and discuss how international intervention (or lack of intervention) from countries like the United States, Canada, and India impacted the confllict in East Pakistan. Debate the role of the international community in conflicts such as this one.

In the Bangladesh Liberation War, Atrocities Were Committed by Both Sides

Secretariat of the International Commission of Jurists

The International Commission of Jurists (ICJ) is an international human rights organization comprised of a commission of sixty eminent jurists. In the following viewpoint, the ICJ's secretariat says that the Pakistan army committed organized killings of Hindus, students, and Bangladeshis throughout Bangladesh. Killings at the University of Dacca were particularly well documented. The ICJ says the killings throughout Bangladesh may have been in the tens or possibly even hundreds of thousands. The Pakistan military, the secretariat says, also deliberately destroyed villages, resulting in a massive refugee crisis. For their part, the secretariat says, Bangladeshis supporting independence committed unorganized but terrible atrocities against ethnic Biharis who opposed independence.

Massive violations of human rights [were] committed over a period of nine months [beginning in March 1971] against the population of East Pakistan by the Pakistan Army aided by the Razakars [a paramilitary force comprised of pro-Pakistan Bangladeshis] and other auxiliary forces.

The principle features of this ruthless oppression were the indiscriminate killing of civilians, including women and children and the poorest and weakest members of the community; the attempt to exterminate or drive out of the country a large part of the Hindu population; the arrest, torture and killing of Awami League activists [supporters of the Bangladesh independence party], students, professional and business men and other potential leaders among the Bengalis; the raping of women; the destruction of villages and towns; and the looting of property. All this was done on a scale which is difficult to comprehend.

The Crackdown in Dacca

President Yahya Khan returned to Karachi on 25 March [1971], and at 10 P.M. that night the army began to leave their cantonment in Dacca. Under the orders of General Tikka Khan the troops unleashed a terrible orgy of killing and destruction, lasting some 48 hours, which came to be known as the army 'crackdown'. An estimated three battalions were used, one armored, one infantry and one artillery.

It is impossible to estimate accurately the numbers of civilian killed in these 48 hours. All that can be said is that they are to be numbered in thousands.

The operation was carefully planned. No shooting began for nearly two hours. The army concentrated on surrounding and occupying strategic points and taking up their positions. The firing began a little before midnight and lasted throughout the night till 6.00 or 7.00 A.M. It was resumed the next day and continued intermittently through the following night and day.

One of the first targets was the University of Dacca, where the attack was directed both at the students and at the University staff. Many of the students who were militant supporters of the Awami League had taken an active part in demonstrations in support of the 'hartal' [strike] and non-cooperation movement.

Warning of the impending attack was received during the evening. The students erected some rather amateurish road-blocks at the entrances to the University campus. These students were unarmed. The attack on the campus started at about one o'clock in the morning. The first attack was directed at Iqbal Hall, which was the centre of the student wing of the Awami League. The army's fire is described as having come from 'all types of arms, mortars, tanks, cannon, machine gun fire and tracer bullets'. The noise was deafening and continued through the night until 7.00 A.M.

After Iqbal Hall, the attack was directed against Salimullah Hall and later at Jagannath Hall, where students belonged to Hindu and other minorities. These Halls were invaded and those students who could not escape were ruthlessly killed. The Halls were set on fire together with a number of other University buildings.

The only place from which any resistance was offered was Iqbal Hall from which came some small arms fire, but this stopped after no more than 35 or 40 minutes. The light nature of the resistance is borne out by the fact that the control centre was heard by several witnesses to enquire over the army radio of the officer leading the attack how many guns had been found in Iqbal Hall. The officer replied 'Only 50 rifles'. He was then ordered to add the number of all rifles and small arms taken in house-to-house searches throughout the city as the recorded number of small arms found at Iqbal Hall.

In addition to attacking the student halls, the army raided the blocks of flats where the University teachers lived. Anthony Mascarenhas, the West Pakistan journalist who was officially attached to the Pakistan Army 9th Division and who later fled to Europe and published a detailed account of the army atrocities, states that he was later told by three separate army officers that the army had lists of people to be liquidated. This is borne out by the fact that only some staff quarters were attacked, but in those which were, the orders appear to have been to kill all adult

Professors, intellectuals, and journalists were among the first to be targeted by the Pakistani army. Many were thrown in mass graves and loosely covered with dirt. © Rolls Press/ Popperfoto/Getty Images.

males. Some people had almost miraculous escapes. Professor Anisur Rahman has given a moving account of how he was saved by having placed a lock on the outside of his door, which led his assailants to think he was away. He and his wife and children crawled about on their hands and knees for some 48 hours in order not to be seen from the ground. In the meantime they heard his colleagues, Professor Guhathakurda and Professor Muniruzzaman dragged out of their flats and shot. It was said afterwards that Professor Muniruzzaman, who spoke Urdu, was shot by accident, and his family was given compensation by the Government.

Those who were able to talk to their assailants in Urdu were often spared. The wife of one lecturer who spoke fluent Urdu was told by a soldier that their orders were to kill everybody, but they found it difficult to carry out the order. Some were spared by pathetic entreaties made by their families.

Altogether ten university teachers were killed, including a renowned Professor of Philosophy, Dr. G. C. Dev. Estimates of the number of students killed vary but seem to have totaled some hundreds. The number would have been higher but for the fact that the University had been closed since March 7 and many students had gone to their homes. A mass grave was dug on the open ground outside the Jagannath and Salimullah Halls. Bodies were collected in trucks from Iqbal Hall and elsewhere on the campus and were thrown into the grave and loosely covered with earth bulldozed into the grave. Some witnesses speak of the sight of arms and legs sticking up out of the grave.

The libraries of the University Halls were burnt out. The Library of the British Council building on the campus was attacked in the mistaken belief that it was the University Library. An eight man Bengali police guard at the British Council premises were shot to death in a small room where they were hiding. A group of about 30 civilians from a nearby slum quarter who had sought refuge on top of one of the blocks of university teachers' flats were similarly wiped out.

Raid on the Old Town

Fearful as was the attack at the University, the greatest slaughter was aimed at the poorest sections of the community living in old parts of the town and in compounds of lightly built huts of bamboo and matting scattered about the city. The raid on the old town began shortly after midnight. Anyone seen on the streets was killed and the sound of firing continued through the night. Twenty taxi drivers who had been sleeping in their taxis on a rank in Victoria Square were killed. A crowd of some 300 coolies [manual laborers] and waiting passengers sheltering in the launch station of the river ferry were wiped out. On the following morning the continuation of the curfew throughout the city was announced on the wireless. Many who had not heard this went out in the morning and were peremptorily shot. During the day of 26 March the army returned in force to the old town and set fire to whole streets and rows of shops. Those attempting to escape were fired at. Among the explanations which have been suggested are that the army thought that this was where the defecting East Bengali soldiers from the army had hidden and that it was in the poorer quarters that the Awami League found its greatest support. The army later described these operations as 'slum clearance'. Whatever the reason, no attempt was made to discriminate. Hindu and Muslim areas alike were set on fire and anyone to be seen on the streets was fired upon.

The areas destroyed in this way included the Hindu temple to Kali Bhari and the two villages where some 2,000 Hindus lived on the Dacca race course; the Hindu areas of Chakri Putti; large areas of 'bustee' houses along the rail track in the old town and near the University, and numerous shopping areas or 'bazaars'. Among those specifically mentioned are Riya Bazaar, Shankari Bazaar, Sakhri Bazaar, tile old timber market, Luxmi Bazaar and Shantinagar Bazaar.

After the first onslaught, the burning and killing continued for some days, directed more specifically against the homes of active Awami League leaders and against Hindus.

Shankhari Patti, a street in the old town, where the conch-shell craftsmen lived, was closed at both ends. Everyone was ordered to leave the houses. Hindus were separated from Muslims, and the Muslims were ordered to return to their houses. The Hindus were then machine gunned to death.

Missionaries who asked why Hindus were being killed were repeatedly told by way of justification 'Hindus are enemies of the state'. Many witnesses testify that the army seemed obsessed with the idea that the movement for autonomy in East Pakistan was inspired by the Hindus, who represented less than 20% of the population. Victims of West Pakistani propaganda, they were erroneously but firmly convinced that the Bengali people in general and the Awami League in particular were dominated by this Hindu element and that they in turn were the agents of India, bent on destroying the Islamic State of Pakistan. It is likely that most Hindus voted for the Awami League in the 1970 elections, but the belief that the Awami League was inspired and run by Hindus was quite false. Its leaders and inspirers were all Muslim, and very few Hindu names appeared among their membership.

Other prime targets of the army during the crack-down were the East Pakistan Rifles and the East Pakistan police. Bengalis in the East Pakistan Rifles had obtained warning of the impending attack on the night of 25 March. They rightly surmised that their compound at Peelkhana near the New Market would be attacked and they warned local residents to leave their homes. Fighting continued for some hours between the West Pakistan and Bengali forces before the Bengalis were overpowered or fled. The police barracks at Rajarbagh were also attacked. In these attacks tanks opened fire first; then troops moved in and leveled the men's sleeping quarters, firing incendiary rounds into the buildings. Not many are believed to have escaped. Police stations throughout the city were also targets for attacks. Hundreds of police and police recruits were killed. A police inspector was reported as saying on the morning of 27 March, 'I am looking for my constables. I have 240 in my district and so far I have only found 30 of them, all dead.' Even the guard at the President's House, who until then had apparently been thought sufficiently loyal to protect President Yahya Khan, were wiped out to a man.

The Biharis [a minority ethnic group] were not slow to join in the attacks on Bengalis. In Mohammedpur, which was predominantly a Bihari area, the houses of Bengalis were raided by armed Biharis on 26 March and the Bengalis were driven out of the area. In the early morning of 26 March a message was intercepted passing over the army radio from the army headquarters to unit commanders throughout the city, congratulating them on the night's work. The message ended, 'You have saved Pakistan'. . . .

On 26 March the radio of the Bangladesh Liberation Army declared Bangladesh a sovereign and independent state, and a call for resistance was made to the Bengali people. With the exception of Sheikh Mujibur Rahman, who waited at his home until arrested at 1:30 A.M., the Awami League leaders escaped and set up a self-proclaimed government of Bangladesh with its headquarters in Calcutta. On the night of March 26 President Yahya Khan in a broadcast to the nation declared that he had ordered the armed forces 'to do their duty and fully restore the authority of the Government'. The Awami League was banned, press censorship was imposed and all political activity forbidden. . . .

Attacks on Biharis and Reprisals

There can be no doubt that in many of these towns where there was a substantial Bihari population, the Bengalis turned against the Biharis during the short period they were in control and some terrible massacres resulted. Among the places where this happened were Chittagong, Khulna, Jessore, Comilla, Rangpur, Phulbari, Dinajpur and Mymensingh. In areas where the non-Bengalis were in a majority, as in some of the railway towns, the Biharis turned and attacked the Bengalis. For example, in Paksey nearly all the Bengalis who had not fled were murdered.

Anthony Mascarenhas has described the attacks on the non-Bengalis in these terms:

Thousands of families of unfortunate Muslims, many of them refugees from Bihar who chose Pakistan at the time of the partition riots in 1947, were mercilessly wiped out. Women were raped, or had their breasts torn out with specially fashioned knives. Children did not escape the horror: the lucky ones were killed with their parents; but many thousands of others must go through what life remains for them with eyes gouged out and limbs amputated. More than 20,000 bodies of non-Bengalis have been found in the main towns, such as Chittagong, Khulna and Jessore. The real toll, I was told everywhere in East Bengal, may have been as high as 100,000, for thousands of non-Bengalis have vanished without a trace. The Government of Pakistan has let the world know about that first horror. What it has suppressed is the second and worse horror which followed when its own army took over the killing. West Pakistan officials privately calculate that altogether both sides have killed 250,000 people.

One may doubt these figures which, like all figures of victims of atrocities, tend to be greatly exaggerated. . . .

It is clear that when the army regained control of these centers, the vengeance wreaked by them and the Biharis upon the Bengali population was horrific.

The army shot, killed and destroyed at sight on the least suspicion, and burnt down village after village, especially those inhabited by Hindus.

The army commander in one town was reported as saying: 'When people start shooting you shoot back. We killed them all. You don't go around counting the bodies of your enemies, you throw them in the rivers and be done with it.'

Hariharpara village near Dacca was turned into an extermination camp. People were brought in trucks and bound together in batches and taken to the river edge where they were made to wade into the water and then shot. The army were assisted by local Biharis who, at the end of the war, fled to Bihari colonies at Mohammedpur, Mirpur and the Adamjee Jute Mill.

Italian missionaries at Jessore have described the mass killings there beginning on April 4. One of them was told by Pakistani soldiers that they had received orders to kill everybody. 'And they did it', he commented, 'men, women, babies. . . . I cannot describe it. It was too terrible. . . .' An Italian priest was walking down a street. Soldiers shouted to him to come over with his hands up. He did so and as he approached they shot him dead. Another priest who witnessed this said, 'They often did it that way'.

Most of the estimates made on both sides of numbers killed are, we believe, much exaggerated and wholly unreliable. The figure of 250,000 quoted above as a Pakistan estimate of the total killed on both sides up to June 1971, may be also be an exaggeration, but it carries with it an implied admission by the Pakistan army with fearsome implications. In March 1972 Mr. Bhutto told an Indian correspondent that the Pakistan estimate of the numbers killed by the army was 40,000 to 50,000. General Tikka Khan told Clare Hollingsworth, the *Daily Telegraph* correspondent, that his estimate of the number killed by the army up to August was 15,000 and for the whole period till December was 30,000. Even these figures are appalling. As Clare Hollingsworth pointed out in reply to General Tikka Khan, 15,000 was the total number killed on both sides in the battle of Alamein, probably the bloodiest battle outside Russia in World War II.

Mascarenhas reported that he was repeatedly told by senior military officers in Dacca and Comilla, 'We are determined to cleanse East Pakistan once and for all of the threat of secession, even if it means killing off two million people and ruling the province as a colony for 30 years.' His evidence is [of] particular value, not only because he heard such remarks made by Pakistan officers when, 'off-guard', but because he made contemporaneous records of the conversations in his diaries, many of which he smuggled out with him. Perhaps the most damning statement of all those he heard was one made by Major-General Shaukat Riza, commanding the 9th Division:

You must be absolutely sure that we have not undertaken such a drastic and expensive operation—expensive both in men and money—for nothing. We have undertaken a job. We are going to finish it, not hand it over half done to the politicians so that they can mess it up again. The army can't keep coming back like this every three or four years. It has a more important task. I assure you that when we have got through with what we are doing there will never be need again for such an operation.

Statements of this kind make clear that the atrocities committed against the population of East Pakistan were part of a deliberate policy by a disciplined force. As such, they differed in character from the mob violence committed at times by Bengalis against Biharis. To quote Anthony Mascarenhas again (from a taped interview):

What struck me was the impression I got, a very hard impression, that this was a regular pattern. It wasn't somebody venting his spleen, but he had clear orders to clean up. It was the pattern of the killing. You killed first Hindus, you killed everyone of the East Pakistan Rifles, the police, or the East Bengal Regiment you found, you killed the students, the male students, and if you got a woman student you probably did something else, the teachers. . . . The teachers are supposed to have been corrupted by the Hindus. It is the pattern that is most frightening. I have seen the partition riots in Delhi in 1947. That was mob frenzy. It was completely different here. This was organized killing; this is what was terrifying about it. It was not being done by mobs. It was a systematic organized thing.

By the middle of May, the army was in full control of the towns of East Pakistan, most of which had been evacuated by more than half their residents and rows of buildings and houses razed to the ground. . . .

It was to escape this terrible slaughter that the refugees fled in millions to the safety of the Indian border. It is estimated that the population of Dacca, a city of well over a million inhabitants, was reduced by some 25%. Jessore, formerly a town of over 100,000 was reduced to about 10,000 by the time of the liberation. A similar exodus occurred from other towns. The population of thousands of destroyed villages fled in their entirety.

The evidence of the massive and indiscriminate destruction of villages is overwhelming. . . .

Refugees and Rape

Another feature on which very many accounts agree is the wholesale rape of women and young girls by Pakistan soldiers. The Bangladesh Government allege that over 70,000 women were made pregnant as a result of these rapes. Whatever the precise numbers, the teams of American and British surgeons carrying out abortions and the widespread government efforts to persuade people to accept these girls into the community, testify to the scale on which raping occurred. The officers turned a blind eye to this savagery, and when challenged denied that it occurred. In many cases the officers themselves kept young girls locked up to serve their pleasure.

The Pakistan Army Perpetrated Widespread Rapes on Bangladeshi Women

Susan Brownmiller

Susan Brownmiller is an American feminist author, journalist, and activist. In the following viewpoint, she describes the widespread rape of Bangladeshi women by Pakistan forces during the 1971 war. Brownmiller reports that hundreds of thousands of women were raped. Brownmiller says that the Bangladesh government portrayed these women as freedom fighters, but nonetheless their husbands and the rest of society often treated them as outcasts. After the rapes, Brownmiller says, Bangladeshi women often suffered from venereal diseases, and those who were pregnant struggled to find safe abortion services. Brownmiller argues that the crisis in Bangladesh was better reported, but not different in kind, from other instances of rape in wartime.

Indira Gandhi's Indian Army had successfully routed the West Pakistanis and had abruptly concluded the war in Bangladesh when small stories hinting at the mass rape of Bengali women began to appear in American newspapers. The first account I read, from the *Los Angeles Times* syndicated service, appeared in the *New York Post* a few days before Christmas, 1971. It reported that the Bangladesh government of Sheik Mujibur Rahman, in recognition of the particular suffering of Bengali women at the hands of Pakistani soldiers, had proclaimed all raped women "heroines" of the war for independence. Farther on in the story came this ominous sentence: "In traditional Bengali village society, where women lead cloistered lives, rape victims often are ostracized."

The Story Gains Creedence

Two days after Christmas a more explicit story, by war correspondent Joseph Fried, appeared in the *New York Daily News....* Fried described the reappearance of young Bengali women on the city streets after an absence of nine months. Some had been packed off to live with relatives in the countryside and others had gone into hiding. "The precautions," he wrote, "proved wise, if not always effective."

A stream of victims and eyewitnesses tell how truckloads of Pakistani soldiers and their hireling razakars [paramilitaries of pro-Pakistan Bengalis] swooped down on villages in the night, rounding up women by force. Some were raped on the spot. Others were carried off to military compounds. Some women were still there when Indian troops battled their way into Pakistani strongholds. Weeping survivors of villages razed because they were suspected of siding with the Mukti Bahini freedom fighters told of how wives were raped before the eyes of their bound husbands, who were then put to death. Just how much of it was the work of Pakistani "regulars" is not clear. Pakistani officers maintain that their men were too disciplined "for that sort of thing."

Fearing I had missed the story in other papers, I put in a call to a friend on the foreign desk of the *New York Times*. "Rape of Bengali women?" He laughed. "I don't think so. It doesn't sound like a *Times* story." A friend at *Newsweek* was similarly skeptical.

Both said they'd keep a lookout for whatever copy passed their way. I got the distinct impression that both men, good journalists, thought I was barking up an odd tree.*

In the middle of January the story gained sudden credence. An Asian relief secretary for the World Council of Churches called a press conference in Geneva to discuss his two-week mission to Bangladesh. The Reverend Kentaro Buma reported that more than 200,000 Bengali women had been raped by Pakistani soldiers during the nine-month conflict, a figure that had been supplied to him by Bangladesh authorities in Dacca. Thousands of the raped women had become pregnant, he said. And by tradition, no Moslem husband would take back a wife who had been touched by another man, even if she had been subdued by force. "The new authorities of Bangladesh are trying their best to break that tradition," Buma informed the newsmen. "They tell the husbands the women were victims and must be considered national heroines. Some men have taken their spouses back home, but these are very, very few."

A story that most reporters couldn't find in Bangladesh was carried by AP and UPI under a Geneva dateline. Boiled down to four paragraphs, it even made the *New York Times*.

Hundreds of Thousands Raped

Organized response from humanitarian and feminist groups was immediate in London, New York, Los Angeles, Stockholm and elsewhere. "It is unthinkable that innocent wives whose lives were virtually destroyed by war are now being totally destroyed by their own husbands," a group of eleven women wrote to the *New York Times* that January. "This . . . vividly demonstrates the blindness of men to injustices they practice against their own women even while struggling for liberation." Galvanized for the first time in history over the issue of rape in war, international

---

* NBC's Liz Trotta was one of the few American reporters to investigate the Bangladesh rape story at this time. She filed a TV report for the weekend news.

aid for Bengali victims was coordinated by alert officials in the London office of the International Planned Parenthood Federation. The Bangladesh government, at first, was most co-operative. In the months to come, the extent of the aggravated plight of the women of Bangladesh during the war for independence would be slowly revealed.

Bengal was a state of 75 million people, officially East Pakistan, when the Bangladesh government declared its independence in March of 1971 with the support of India. Troops from West Pakistan were flown to the East to put down the rebellion. During the nine-month terror, terminated by the two-week armed intervention of India, a possible three million persons lost their lives, ten million fled across the border to India, and 200,000, 300,000 or possibly 400,000 women (three sets of statistics have been variously quoted) were raped. Eighty percent of the raped women were Moslems, reflecting the population of Bangladesh, but Hindu and Christian women were not exempt. As Moslems, most Bengali women were used to living in purdah, strict, veiled isolation that includes separate, secluded shelter arrangements apart from men, even in their own homes. The Pakistanis were also Moslem, but there the similarity stopped. Despite a shared religious heritage, Punjabi Pakistanis are taller, lighter-skinned and "rawboned" compared to dark, small-boned Bengalis. This racial difference would provide added anguish to those Bengali women who found themselves pregnant after their physical ordeal.

Hit-and-run rape of large numbers of Bengali women was brutally simple in terms of logistics as the Pakistani regulars swept through and occupied the tiny, populous land, an area little larger than the state of New York. (Bangladesh is the most overcrowded country in the world.) The Mukti Bahini "freedom fighters" were hardly an effective counterforce. According to victims, Moslem Biharis who collaborated with the Pakistani Army—the hireling *razakars*—were most enthusiastic rapists. In the general breakdown of law and order, Mukti Bahini themselves committed rape, a situation reminiscent of World War II when Greek and Italian peasant women became victims of whatever soldiers happened to pass through their village.

One Incident

Aubrey Menen, sent on a reporting assignment to Bangladesh, reconstructed the *modus operandi* of one hit-and-run rape. With more than a touch of romance the Indian Catholic novelist chose as his archetypal subject a seventeen-year-old Hindu bride of one month whom he called "the belle of the village." Since she was, after all, a ravished woman, Menen employed his artistic license to paint a sensual picture of her "classical buttocks": ". . . they were shaped, that is, as the great Sanskrit poet Kalidasa had prescribed, like two halves of a perfect melon."

Menen got his information from the victim's father. Pakistani soldiers had come to the little village by truck one day in October. Politely and thoroughly they searched the houses—"for pamphlets," they said. Little talk was exchanged since the soldiers spoke a language no one in the village could understand. The bride of one month gave a soldier a drink of coconut juice, "in peace."

At ten o'clock that night the truckload of soldiers returned, waking the family by kicking down the door of their corrugated iron house. There were six soldiers in all, and the father said that none of them was drunk. I will let Menen tell it:

> Two went into the room that had been built for the bridal couple. The others stayed behind with the family, one of them covering them with his gun. They heard a barked order, and the bridegroom's voice protesting. Then there was silence until the bride screamed. Then there was silence again, except for some muffled cries that soon subsided.
>
> In a few minutes one of the soldiers came out, his uniform in disarray. He grinned to his companions. Another soldier took his place in the extra room. And so on, until all the six had raped the belle of the village. Then all six left, hurriedly.

The father found his daughter lying on the string cot unconscious and bleeding. Her husband was crouched on the floor, kneeling over his vomit.

After interviewing the father, Menen tracked down the young woman herself in a shelter for rape victims in Dacca. She was, he reported, "truly beautiful," but he found her mouth "strange." It was hard and tense. The young woman doubted that she would ever return to her tiny village. Her husband of one month had refused to see her and her father, she said, was "ashamed." The villagers, too, "did not want me." The conversation, Menen wrote, proceeded with embarrassing pauses, but it was not without high tension.

> I took my leave. I was at the door when she called me back.
> "Huzoor," a title of honour.
> "Yes?"
> "You will see that those men are punished," she said.
> "Punished. Punished. *Punished*."

Systematic Abuse

Menen's report on the belle of the village was artfully drawn, but it did dramatize the plight of thousands of raped and rejected Bengali women. Other observers with a less romantic eye provided more realistic case studies. Rape in Bangladesh had hardly been restricted to beauty. Girls of eight and grandmothers of seventy-five had been sexually assaulted during the nine-month repression. Pakistani soldiers had not only violated Bengali women on the spot; they abducted tens of hundreds and held them by force in their military barracks for nightly use. The women were kept naked to prevent their escape. In some of the camps, pornographic movies were shown to the soldiers, "in an obvious attempt to work the men up," one Indian writer reported.

Khadiga, thirteen years old, was interviewed by a photojournalist in Dacca. She was walking to school with four other girls when they were kidnapped by a gang of Pakistani soldiers. All five were put in a military brothel in Mohammedpur and held captive for six months until the end of the war. Khadiga was regularly abused by two men a day; others, she said, had to service seven to ten men daily. (Some accounts have mentioned as many as eighty assaults in a single night, a bodily abuse that is beyond my ability to fully comprehend, even as I write these words.) At first, Khadiga said, the soldiers tied a gag around her mouth to keep her from screaming. As the months wore on and the captives' spirit was broken, the soldiers devised a simple *quid pro quo.* They withheld the daily ration of food until the girls had submitted to the full quota.

Kamala Begum, a wealthy widow, lived in a Dacca suburb. When the fighting started she sent her two daughters into the countryside to hide. She felt she could afford to stay behind, secure in her belief that she was "too old" to attract attention. She was assaulted by three men, two Pakistanis and one razakar, in her home.

Khadiga and Kamala Begum were interviewed by Bérengère d'Aragon, a woman photographer, in a Dacca abortion clinic.

Rape, abduction and forcible prostitution during the nine-month war proved to be only the first round of humiliation for the Bengali women. Prime Minister Mujibur Rahman's declaration that victims of rape were national heroines was the opening shot of an ill-starred campaign to reintegrate them into society— by smoothing the way for a return to their reluctant husbands or by finding bridegrooms for the unmarried ones from among his Mukti Bahini freedom fighters. Imaginative in concept for a country in which female chastity and purdah isolation are cardinal principles, the "marry them off" campaign never got off the ground. Few prospective bridegrooms stepped forward, and those who did made it plain that they expected the government, as father figure, to present them with handsome dowries.

"The demands of the men have ranged from the latest model of Japanese car, painted red, to the publication of unpublished poems," a government official bitterly complained. Another stumbling block, perhaps unexpected by the Bangladeshis, was the attitude of the raped women. "Many won't be able to tolerate the presence of a man for some time," the same official admitted.

Venereal Disease and Pregnancy

But more pressing concerns than marriage had to be faced. Doctors sent to Bangladesh by International Planned Parenthood discovered that gynecological infection was rampant. "Almost every rape victim tested had a venereal disease," an Australian physician told the *New York Times*.

The most serious crisis was pregnancy. Accurate statistics on the number of raped women who found themselves with child were difficult to determine but 25,000 is the generally accepted figure. Less speculative was the attitude of the raped, pregnant women. Few cared to bear their babies. Those close to birth expressed little interest in the fate of the child. In addition to an understandable horror of rearing a child of forcible rape, it was freely acknowledged in Bangladesh that the bastard children with their fair Punjabi features would never be accepted into Bengali culture—and neither would their mothers.

Families with money were able to send their daughters to expert abortionists in Calcutta, but shame and self-loathing and lack of alternatives led to fearsome, irrational solutions in the rural villages. Dr. Geoffrey Davis of the London-based International Abortion Research and Training Center who worked for months in the remote countryside of Bangladesh reported that he had heard of "countless" incidents of suicide and infanticide during his travels. Rat poison and drowning were the available means. Davis also estimated that five thousand women had managed to abort themselves by various indigenous methods, with attendant medical complications.

A Catholic convent in Calcutta, Mother Theresa's, opened its doors in Dacca to women who were willing to offer their babies for overseas adoption, but despite the publicity accorded to Mother Theresa, few rape victims actually came to her shelter. Those who learned of the option chose to have an abortion. Planned Parenthood, in cooperation with the newly created Bangladesh Central Organization for Women's Rehabilitation, set up clinics in Dacca and seventeen outlying areas to cope with the unwanted pregnancies. In its first month of operation the Dacca clinic alone, reported doing more than one hundred terminations.

Torture

The Bangladesh Central Organization for Women's Rehabilitation, created by Bengali women themselves, proved to be a heroic moving force. In a country with few women professionals, those who had the skills stepped forward to help their victimized sisters. One, a doctor, Helena Pasha, who admitted that prior to the war she had thoroughly disapproved of abortion, gave freely of her time and services with little monetary compensation. Women social workers like Tahera Shafiq took over the organizational work and gave aid and comfort that the traumatized rape victims could not accept from men. Tahera Shafiq was adamant on one point. Rape or forcible prostitution were false, inadequate words to describe what the Bengali women had gone through. She preferred in conversation to use the word "torture."

Rehabilitation meant more than comfort, tenderness and abortion. The women's organization sought to train the homeless, rejected women in working skills. Handicrafts, shorthand and typing were the obvious choices—small steps until one remembers that most of the women had never been outside their rural villages before. The hoped-for long-range goal of "rehabilitation" still remained marriage. "An earning woman has better prospects of marriage than others," one social worker said dryly. But for many of the tortured women, aid and succor arrived too late, or not at all. "Alas, we have reports of some who have landed in brothels," a male government official acknowledged. "It is a terrible tragedy."

As the full dimensions of the horror became known, those who looked for rational, military explanations returned again and again to the puzzle of why the mass rapes had taken place. "And a campaign of terror includes rape?" Aubrey Menen prodded a Bengali politician. He got a reflective answer. "What do soldiers talk about in barracks? Women and sex," the politician mused. "Put a gun in their hands and tell them to go out and frighten the wits out of a population and what will be the first thing that leaps to their mind?" Fearing the magnitude of his own answer, the politician concluded, "Remember, some of our Bengali women are very beautiful." Mulk Raj Anand, an Indian novelist, was convinced of conspiracy. The rapes were so systematic and pervasive that they had to be conscious Army policy, "planned by the West Pakistanis in a deliberate effort to create a new race" or to dilute Bengali nationalism, Anand passionately told reporters.

Theory and conjecture abounded, all of it based on the erroneous assumption that the massive rape of Bangladesh had been a crime without precedent in modern history.

War and Rape

But the mass rape of Bangladesh had not been unique. The number of rapes per capita during the nine-month occupation of Bangladesh had been no greater than the incidence of rape during one month of occupation in the city of Nanking in 1937, no greater than the per capita incidence of rape in Belgium and France as the German Army marched unchecked during the first three months of World War I, no greater than the violation of women in every village in Soviet Russia in World War II. A "campaign of terror" and a charge of "conscious Army policy" had been offered up in explanation by seekers of rational answers in those wars as well, and later forgotten.

The story of Bangladesh was unique in one respect. For the first time in history the rape of women in war, and the complex aftermath of mass assault, received serious international attention. The desperate need of Sheik Mujibur Rahman's government for international sympathy and financial aid was part of the reason; a new feminist consciousness that encompassed rape as a political issue and a growing, practical acceptance of abortion as a solution to unwanted pregnancy were contributing factors of critical importance. And so an obscure war in an obscure corner of the globe, to Western eyes, provided the setting for an examination of the "unspeakable" crime. For once, the particular terror of unarmed women facing armed men had full hearing.

A Refugee Crisis Pulled India into the Bangladesh Conflict

Kalyan Chaudhuri

Kalyan Chaudhuri was an Indian journalist; his grandfather was killed in the East Pakistan conflict. In the following viewpoint, he says that Pakistani atrocities in East Pakistan caused a massive wave of Bangladeshi refugees to flee East Pakistan into India. He argues that the situation created a massive problem for India, which was forcibly involved in East Pakistan affairs because of the refugee crisis on its border. Chaudhuri says that accusations by Pakistan that India was preventing Bangladeshis from returning home were nonsense; in fact, he says, Bangladeshis feared returning to their homes. Chaudhuri also reports on the terrible conditions of disease and starvation in many of the refugee camps.

There is no doubt that the aim of the military pogrom [an organized attack on innocent people] of 1971 [by West Pakistan] was to drive the Easterners out of East Pakistan. In the wake of the killing, first in cities and towns and then in the countryside, Bengalis left their homes convinced once and for all that East Pakistan could not or would not offer them the simple

Kalyan Chaudhuri, *Genocide in Bangladesh*. Andhra Pradesh, India: Orient Longman, 1972, pp. 68–75. Copyright © 1972 by Orient Longman Ltd. All rights reserved. Reproduced by permission.

guarantees of security of life and property that should have been their inalienable rights as citizens in their own country.

The Exodus

The exodus began from early April, and in millions, for at least a safe shelter in neighbouring places on the other side of the border in Indian territory. It continued for eight months. As the army fanned out in the villages and intensified their systematic operations on the plea of combing out the rebels who were consolidating their strength for armed struggle to create an independent Republic of Bangladesh, terrified people poured daily into bordering areas of India.

The rebel Bangladesh Government which was formed on April 10, 1971, in the liberated area of Mujibnagar of Kushtia district, close to the Indian border and the Government of India have since been accused of playing up the magnitude of the massacre. No playing up, however, was necessary. The facts spoke for themselves. Andre Malraux: called it "a pogrom of genocidal proportions". . . .

Taking over the charge of military operations in East Pakistan in March, General Tikka Khan boasted of "erasing a race of bastards in Bangladesh", by destroying their "Hinduite culture" and teaching them how to be "true Mussalmans".

Following the pattern of the army operations it becomes clear that the plans were: to cleanse the eastern colony of all non-Muslims, especially Hindus, kill off or push out enough Bengali Muslims and induct in their place enough 'loyal' Pakistanis so as to reduce the Bengalis to a minority, thus rendering Bengali nationalism ineffective; snuff out the finest cultural renaissance ever to appear in the Muslim world, bury secularism deep in the graves of the Bengali patriots and re-establish military dictatorship over East Pakistan.

Visitors to the bordering areas in West Bengal in those days must have seen the enormous influx of refugees coming daily from the other side and huge camps of displaced persons living on charity.

Dhaka war refugees await an evacuation bus to India. The massive influx of Bangladeshi refugees was a deciding factor in India's participation in the war. © AP Images/Michael Laurent.

By the end of April, one month after the army operation had started, there was an estimated one million refugees inside Indian territory. In the main these were not Muslims but minority Hindus. The speed of the influx was tremendous. By the end of May, the refugee wave had swelled to an estimated three-and-a-half million and the figure of Muslims rose high.

Forced to Be Involved

Despite the Pakistan Government's accusation that India had been interfering in its internal affairs and China's charge that she [Indian prime minister Indira Gandhi] had been spreading cooked-up stories of refugees for political gains, India opened the border for the fleeing evacuees. During her world tour in September, 1971, Mrs Indira Gandhi admitted that India was forced to be involved in Pakistani affairs because of the tremendous financial and socio-economic burden imposed by the huge influx. She said, "Only bullets could have prevented the terrorised fleeing people from crossing over the border. India did not like to do it."

The Guardian of London wrote on September 10: "No nation, or world community can realistically be expected to succour nine million refugees indefinitely. . . . West Bengal's camps of squalor represent, starkly, a country in tatters, the rubble of a united Pakistan. These refugees are not the result of some unimaginable natural phenomenon. They are the direct result of political and military action."

As the extent and gravity of the refugee crisis emerged, the International Rescue Committee sent in early June a mission of five volunteer leaders to India, headed by Mr Angier Bidde Duke, its chairman. The object of the mission was to obtain a first-hand picture of the situation, and to initiate an emergency programme for the refugees, the professionals in particular.

The report submitted to the IRC by the Emergency Mission on July 28 stated that six million Bengalis, Muslims, Hindus, Buddhists and Christians, had streamed out of East Pakistan, their homeland, to the bordering states of West Bengal, Assam, Tripura and Meghalaya. Thousands on thousands of new refugees were arriving every day, and the pressures on India generated by this multitude of destitute refugees were mounting dangerously.

The findings of the IRC's Mission to India through interviews with fleeing refugees revealed that the mass terror unleashed by the West Pakistan army in East Pakistan was continuing with unabated savagery. People were being taken out of their houses and machine-gunned in cities and the countryside. Men, women and children were being bayoneted to death, women raped. The figure of deaths available to the Mission in June was 200,000.

By June 15, the refugee population in India reached 5–8 million, of whom close to two-thirds were housed in camps of all descriptions in [the Indian states of] Assam, Tripura and Meghalaya. Figures prepared by the Indian Government show that nearly one-third, mostly Hindus and upper-class Muslims who had friends and relatives, stayed outside the camps.

Reports of the IRC Mission, Red Cross, Caritas, Oxfam, Ramkrishna Mission, Bharat Sevasram Sangha and other social welfare organisations who were conducting relief work in refugee camps suggested that their number had gone up to six million by the end of June. Nearly one million huddled in shelters built in bush on the outskirts of the bordering villages of India. Soon the Indian Government, with the assistance of some international voluntary organisations, set up a chain of refugee camps where the homeless could at least have a share of a roof and a meal a day. Many camps were set up in empty schools and colleges.

The influx continued. But with the outbreak of cholera in early June, news of which spread in East Pakistan, the border crossings slowed down. But, the IRC Mission reported, once the threat from cholera subsided, thousands again began to pour over every night, despite the air of tension the Pakistani army had tried to maintain on the border by mortar fire. There was no indication that the exodus had been halted. "If the present trend continues, the figure is likely to go up to seven million before July is out. Seven million people is the total population of Cuba", said the Mission.

The Situation Worsens

The refugees, many of whom had walked distances of up to 150 miles, appeared to have travelled from cities and villages relatively near the Indian border. There were unquestionably large numbers of Easterners who were unable to escape because of their more central location within East Pakistan. They came to

INFLUX OF REFUGEES FROM EAST PAKISTAN INTO INDIA SINCE THE PARTITION OF INDIA AND PAKISTAN IN 1947		
Name of Indian State	Between 1947 Partition and February 1971	Between March 25, 1971 and December 15, 1971
Assam	701,000	316,000
Bihar	---	9,000
Meghalaya	---	668,000
Tripura	517,000	1,415,000
West Bengal	4,013,000	7,491,000
Total	5,231,000	9,899,000

Taken from: Kalyan Chaudhuri, *Genocide in Bangladesh*, New Delhi, India: Orient Longman, 1972, p. 94.

India initially by crossing the border and along roads normally travelled. With the closure of the border by the military, large numbers continued to infiltrate through the 1300-mile border with India, through forests and swamps. These groups, with numbers sometimes up to 50,000 in a 24-hour period, for the most part settled along the major routes in India. They were found wherever there was a combination of available ground and minimal water supply. Many of them avoided camp communities and 'melted' into the countryside. The camps varied in size from small groups to upwards of 50,000.

The shelter, when it existed, was of three main types—small thatched huts made of locally available material, small low tents made from wood frames covered with tarpaulin and, where available, cement casement and drainage pipes. Sanitary facilities in the camps were almost non-existent. The inadequate drainage system, the shallow wells and poor sanitation made gross contamination an obvious sequence and ultimately cholera broke out. Diarrhoea, skin diseases and gastro-enteritis also broke out.

The combination of the monsoon [high seasonal rains], deficient health facilities and the influx of new refugees made an upswing in the cholera incidence in camps, especially located in the Khasi-Jaintia hills of Meghalaya, close to Sylhet, under one of the heaviest rainfall areas of Cherapunji. In the camp hospitals in those areas cholera was a common feature. International welfare organisations reported that nearly 10,000 refugees died of cholera and gastro-enteritis and from malnutrition and exposure to monsoon rains between May and July. Fortunately the first outbreak of cholera was controlled with the help of voluntary agencies.

Despite continuous attempts by the international community, no political solution could be found for the return of the refugees to East Pakistan. Delegates, political leaders, [and] legislative members from all over the world toured the camps and went back with the same impression that the refugees, despite their human sufferings in the camps, would not go back unless they were freed of the fear which had prompted them to flee.

On June 8 General Tikka Khan told a team of British MPs [members of Parliament] in Islamabad that India was obstructing the return of refugees. He said that left to themselves 99 per cent of the refugees would come back. Asked why they had not done so in spite of the Pakistan President's appeal to them, he replied that India was applying force to prevent them from coming back. When an MP remarked, "You are not being serious", the General said, "No, I am serious."

There was no evidence to support the allegation. The United Nations High Commissioner for Refugees, Prince Sadruddin Aga Khan, who claimed himself not "pro-Pakistan" nor "pro-India" but "pro-refugees" was repeatedly asked by representatives of the world press to find out if there was any truth in the

Pakistan Government's allegation. But the result of his inquiry could not satisfy the Government of Pakistan. After a tour of the refugee camps along the border line of India and the East Pakistan countryside in June, the Prince categorically said that there was no evidence that the Indian Government had obstructed the return of refugees. Again in Paris on July 10, the Prince in reply to a question said that it would not be logical to say that India was in any way holding back their return. On July 19, at Kathmandu, two volunteers of the British organisation, "War on Want", described as "rubbish" the Pakistani allegation. At Calcutta on July 22, Mr Manfred Cross, an Australian MP, described it as "impossible".

Mr Toby Jessel, of the four-man British Parliamentary delegation, on his arrival in London after a tour in India and Pakistan in late June told newsmen that the refugees were still scared and unwilling to go back to East Pakistan "unless it is safe". . . .

Living Skeletons

Before June the enormous problem faced by India because of the never-ending flow of refugees remained almost unknown to the world public. In the middle of June, Ms Alexandra Metcalfe, Vice-Chairman, Save the Children Fund, visited refugee camps on a 15-day fact-finding tour. What she saw disquieted her. Simultaneously some foreign journalists were reporting from four refugee-ridden States of India and they, with their cameramen, saw the story for what it was. In the last days of June the first pictures of small children reduced to living skeletons hit the pages of the Western newspapers. People of the world saw on television dead bodies being eaten by dogs in open fields.

In her press statement in *The Times*, London, on July, 1971, Lady Alexandra Metcalfe reported that the refugee situation was going to deteriorate rapidly, epidemics of all sorts spread like wild fire threatening the life of hundreds of thousands. The stories that appeared in the newspapers were first widely believed to be mere "Indian propaganda" until teams of British MPs, like John

Stonehouse, Arthur Bottomley and Reginald Prentice and U.S. Senators like Edward Kennedy, J.W. Fulbright and William B. Saxbe had drawn world attention to the army atrocities "of genocidal proportions" and the misery of refugees.

Canadian Neutrality on East Pakistan Was Morally Dubious

Richard Pilkington

Richard Pilkington is a doctoral candidate at the University of Toronto. In the following viewpoint, he says that Canada maintained a policy of neutrality during the 1971 East Pakistan crisis. Pilkington writes that Canada did not want to damage its relationship with Pakistan or encourage separatist movements because of its own separatist movement in Quebec. Pilkington concludes that Canada could not have done much to prevent the atrocities in East Pakistan, but the nation's stance was ethically dubious and showed a lack of concern for human rights and democracy.

D rawing upon recently declassified materials from the Canadian government archives, this article investigates how and why Canada formulated its response to the East Pakistan crisis of 1971. As a provider of substantial amounts of development aid and as a partner in Pakistan's nuclear power programme, Ottawa [the Canadian capital] had established an important relationship with Islamabad [the capital of Pakistan]. Despite knowledge of the atrocities in East Pakistan, the Canadian government

Richard Pilkington, "In the National Interest? Canada and the East Pakistan Crisis of 1971," *Journal of Genocide Research*, 2011, pp. 451–474. Copyright © 2011 by Taylor & Francis Group. All rights reserved. Reproduced by permission of the publisher and author.

chose not to exert hard influence by threatening the withdrawal
of aid or technical assistance, but to adopt a four-strand policy
based upon public neutrality, the private encouragement of a political settlement in South Asia, calls for restraint to both India
and Pakistan, and the provision of humanitarian relief. This approach served to protect Canada's relationship with Pakistan,
deemed desirable in terms of national interest, narrowly construed, and maintained Canadian neutrality with regard to a foreign secessionist issue that might have stirred unwelcome comparisons with its own separatist debate over Quebec [a Canadian
province that had agitated for independence]. . . .

The Global Background

Before discussing and analyzing the Canadian response in de-
tail, it is first necessary to situate the East Pakistan crisis within
three layers of background context: domestic, regional and
global. Domestically, the two wings of Pakistan were culturally
dissimilar. Their populations spoke different languages, shared
different histories and embraced different forms of Islam. In addition, 1,000 miles of Indian territory separated the wings, and
their economies and markets were distinct. Upon partition, West
Pakistan came to dominate the executive, the bureaucracy and the
military, and the benefits of this regional bias of power became
manifest in increasing inter-wing economic disparity. By 1971,
military dictators had ruled Pakistan for over a decade. However,
Yahya [Khan, president of Pakistan] had promised elections and
a transition to democratic government. To the surprise of many,
the Awami League, a political party of the more populous East,
won a majority of seats in the proposed new assembly. The threat
of a power shift from the West to the East created an impasse, and
Yahya postponed the opening of the new body. Consequently,
the Awami League made increasing demands for regional autonomy, which the West perceived as moves towards secession. In
response, the West attempted to terrorize East Pakistan into sub-
mission, committing mass atrocities against what it considered

potential sources of organized resistance and Hindus generally, whom Islamabad perceived as subversive.

The developments in East Pakistan played out against a background of regional tension. In South Asia, Hindu-Muslim intercommunal violence at partition had led to deep mistrust between India and Pakistan; mistrust reinforced by two subsequent wars over Kashmir [a region split between Indian and Pakistan control] and ongoing clashes at the line of control. Consequently, India and Pakistan perceived each other as enemies ready to exploit weaknesses.

Globally, as the US pursued a policy of Cold War containment, India remained officially non-aligned, but in receipt of substantial Soviet military aid. By contrast, Pakistan became a key US ally in Asia and benefited from heavy US economic and military investment. However, when Pakistan used US weapons in the Indo-Pakistan War of 1965, Washington stopped military supply. In addition, it reduced its economic aid to Islamabad, although this remained significant. The curtailment of US military supplies caused Pakistan to seek support elsewhere and it needed look no further than neighbouring China, which shared a mutual dislike of India, with whom it had itself warred in 1962. Islamabad and Beijing became allied in Asia. . . .

The Crisis

The clampdown in East Pakistan came as a surprise to Canada and to the international community as a whole. Although Canada maintained no permanent representation in the East, [Canadian high commissioner to Islamabad, John] Small made regular visits from Islamabad to oversee development initiatives. During mid-March 1971, the high commissioner paid such a call and reported to Ottawa that, owing to 'overwhelming autonomist sentiment' and the severe limitations on the West Pakistani-dominated army's ability to impose national unity, he 'doubt[ed] any agreed solution [could] be found', and believed the most likely outcome to be the independence of the East. However,

Foreign Service Officers Criticize US Neutrality in the East Pakistan Conflict

Our government has failed to denounce the suppression of democracy. Our government has failed to denounce atrocities. Our government has failed to take forceful measures to protect its citizens while at the same time bending over backwards to placate the West Pak[istan] dominated government and to lessen any deservedly negative international public relations impact against them. Our government has evidenced what many will consider moral bankrupt, (. . .) But we have chosen not to intervene, even morally, on the grounds that the Awami conflict, in which unfortunately the overworked term genocide is applicable, is purely an internal matter of a sovereign state. Private Americans have expressed disgust. We, as professional civil servants, express our dissent with current policy and fervently hope that our true and lasting interests here can be defined and our policies redirected.

Archer Blood, "U.S. Consulate (Dacca) Cable,
Dissent from US Policy toward East Pakistan,"
April 6, 1971.

talks held between Yahya and Mujibur Rahman, head of the Awami League political party and democratically elected leader of both the East and the country as a whole, soon appeared to be leading to some form of agreement. Thus, as he left to return to Islamabad on 20 March, Small, in common with many observers around the world, was optimistic that, despite the odds, a solution was indeed imminent.

Such widely shared optimism proved somewhat misplaced, as Islamabad ordered the commencement of a campaign of military oppression against sections of the civilian population in the East, commencing on 25 March. Initial reports from Dhaka [in East Pakistan] were unclear. In the absence of any permanent Canadian representation and of foreign reporters, whom the army had quickly rounded up and shipped to Karachi, the fog of war descended. As the Awami League described the 'cold blooded army killing of unarmed civilians', Islamabad insisted that the military was simply restoring order and that the situation was very much in hand. Indeed, on 31 March, Yahya wrote to [Canadian prime minister Pierre] Trudeau explaining that the situation in East Pakistan was 'well under control' and accounts to the contrary were misleading. Small observed, however, that censorship made reports in West Pakistani newspapers 'worthless' and that official releases were highly questionable. Despite the deliberate interruption of telex and telephone communications with the East, eyewitnesses began relaying reports of the use of tanks, machine guns and flame-throwers in Dhaka, and attacks on the Awami League offices, the old city, university residences and Hindu shrines. The small East Pakistani military and police forces had been 'disarmed, dispersed or rounded up', with many killed and wounded. Bodies lay in the streets.

In the absence of concrete information, and not wishing to act precipitously, the Canadian government prevaricated. In response to questions in the House of Commons on 2 April, [Canadian secretary of state for external affairs Mitchell] Sharp observed, 'We do not yet have the facts'. He continued by noting that the situation was unclear, intervention might not help, and that Canada was ready to assist in humanitarian efforts. Initially highly justifiable, given the need to establish what was really happening in East Pakistan and to formulate a response based on proper consideration rather than display a knee-jerk reaction, Sharp's first public statement already loosely embraced two threads of what would ultimately evolve into a four-strand Canadian policy. One was that of public neutrality during the crisis, another the application of the balm of humanitarian relief, which would serve to treat the symptoms of the problem, but not the underlying cause.

As events unfolded, reports of atrocities continued to flow and a battle to influence Canadian policy developed between the high commissioners in Islamabad and New Delhi, Small's views ultimately holding the greatest sway. In the absence of representation in Dhaka, Ottawa and Small turned to the British for further information. The UK confirmed to the Canadian high commission in London that 'Awami League supporters generally seem to have been hunted down', and 'the Hindus, in particular, have apparently been slaughtered in large numbers'. Although the army itself had almost stopped shooting people in Dhaka, non-Bengalis were 'on the rampage, with the army turning a blind eye'. In addition, the British high commissioner to Islamabad informed Small that the army had exterminated members of the small East Pakistani military and police forces in Dhaka, the latter being buried in a commercial dump. West Pakistani troops had 'laid [the] university waste', many bodies there having been bulldozed into a mass grave.

Maintaining Neutrality

Despite the ongoing influx of atrocity reports, Sharp maintained the developing Canadian position of neutrality, exhibiting an impressive ability in obfuscation in the House of Commons. On 7 April, five days after receiving the telegrams referred to above, in response to a question as to whether the government had received any news about mass killings in East Pakistan, Sharp insisted: 'I have no information *directly* from any representative of the Canadian government'. Having employed this deft sidestep, he continued by admitting that there was undoubtedly a good deal of bloodshed and denounced 'violence on *both* sides'. He concluded: 'I do not think pious declarations against violence are going to achieve anything. We are searching for some means by which we can be constructive, by supplying relief or something of that kind'.

As Sharp remained evasive in public, the formulation of Canadian policy continued behind the scenes. In his very first communication after the clampdown, Small had made it clear that he now believed there was 'no hope of reconciliation'. As he had explained further on 6 April, given the inadequate size of the army in the East and its consequent inability to control the vast rural population beyond the main urban centres, 'I cannot visualize discovery of any Bengalis of stature or with sufficient following who could now be found to bear the odium of dealing with their oppressors. The Pak[istan] of . . . Jinnah [the founder of Pakistan] is dead. In the absence of viable military or political solutions, Small believed independence, in time, was inevitable. Noting the adverse reaction in Islamabad to early condemnation of its actions by Moscow and New Delhi, on 8 April, Small argued that to remain on good terms with Islamabad and 'aloof from re-criminations and quarrels between Indian and Pakistan, Canada should adopt an approach that was non-committal or neutral. He contended that Canada should consider the clamp-down an internal matter for Pakistan to address, and should express humanitarian concern over the effect of events on the Pakistani economy, Canadian aid programmes and any hardships endured by all those in the East.

Small's opinion was of particular importance as, more than his counterpart in New Delhi, he had the ears of the key actors in Ottawa. On 29 March, the under-secretary of state for external affairs, Edgar Ritchie, had written a personal letter to the high commissioner to Islamabad offering congratulations on the lat-ter's 'excellent reporting', which had been noted by Trudeau him-self. A month later, Small's analytical abilities were again praised in a memorandum from [Canadian foreign policy adviser Ivan] Head to the prime minister. However, Small's opinions were not shared by [Canadian high commissioner James] George in New Delhi, which became apparent as Ottawa attempted to formulate policy in advance of replying to Yahya's letter of 31 March.

George believed the soft policy proposed by Small to be lack-ing in moral fibre and 'much too gentle'. Without suggesting spe-cific steps, he countered: 'Are we going to gloss over [the] fact that majority (75 million) is being suppressed by minority (55 million)? Are issues only legal and constitutional or also political and moral?' Nevertheless, and somewhat in contradiction of his questions above, George admitted that Canada should temporarily maintain 'a low profile' until it was able to 'see more clearly'. Meanwhile, it should occupy the safe ground of expressing 'humanitarian concern [and] plea[s] for restraint and peaceful (i.e. political) settlement'.

Small hit back strongly in response to George's criticism. He maintained that Canada should 'distinguish between rumours and emotions . . . on the one hand and facts and genuine [Canadian] interests on the other'. To the high commissioner in Islamabad, such national interests centred less on the overt promotion of Canadian democratic values abroad, and more on Canada's realist 'primary interest' of maintaining good relations through an ongoing programme of Pakistani development assistance. In addressing George's point about ethical principle, Small twice labelled the former's response as emotional, while continuing to present his own judgment as based on the firm foundation of reason. Questioning the propaganda of the Awami League and New Delhi, as well as that of Islamabad, he observed that 'while much blood has tragically flowed, loose talk of genocide must be discounted'. Six days after Small delivered this riposte, Head wrote to Trudeau, attaching sections of Small's telegram and stating: 'It is one of a continuing series of reports of a remarkably high caliber which he [Small] has been filing in the past two months on the subject of Pakistan's internal difficulties'. Head did not go to the trouble of attaching George's telegram, nor did he fail to note Small's comments about the high commissioner in New Delhi. The prime minister's close foreign policy adviser observed that George had argued 'somewhat emotionally'. Conveniently, whether by chance or design, Small had recommended a course of action that fitted neatly with the more general foreign policy goals of the Canadian government: focus on the promotion of national interest, narrowly interpreted, and adherence to neutrality in the face of separatist issues overseas. . . .

Canadian Policy Comprised Four Strands

Canadian policy during the crisis comprised four strands: first, the maintenance of public impartiality with regard to the respective positions of East and West Pakistan and those of Islamabad and New Delhi; second, the encouragement, through soft private influence, of Islamabad in its seeking a domestic political solution; third, the urging of restraint upon both India and Pakistan; and, fourth, the provision of humanitarian relief to the East Pakistani victims. In refusing to condemn the action of Islamabad publicly and privately, and in maintaining the ongoing development aid programme, Canada sought to maintain its sway in Pakistan in the longer term and to facilitate the second policy strand, that of being . . . able to exert soft influence upon the West Pakistani leaders. The third strand aimed to encourage a reduction in tension on the subcontinent to provide time for a viable political solution to be found. The remaining strand sought to reduce the suffering of the victims, but addressed the symptoms of the problem rather than the underlying cause. By drawing down the veil of sovereignty over what it portrayed as a domestic issue, Ottawa was better able to protect itself from demands for firmer action. This combination of initiatives was publicly presented to portray Canada as taking a caring and responsible, if pragmatic and realistic approach, to a serious international problem. Conveniently, this stance also served to protect Ottawa's ongoing and future relationship with Islamabad, deemed desirable in terms of national interest, narrowly construed, and maintained Canadian neutrality with regard to a foreign secessionist issue that might have stirred unwelcome comparisons with its own separatist debate over Quebec. In these respects, the policy was successful.

Nevertheless, there were two disadvantages to this approach. First, in failing to discontinue aid, or at the very least publicly or privately condemning Islamabad, Ottawa adopted the moral low ground on an issue in which a military dictatorship was attempting to maintain power, by denying democratically elected representatives their right to govern and by perpetrating systematic atrocities and gross human rights abuses. Second, with regard to encouraging a peaceful settlement in South Asia, the policy was inherently flawed from the outset, a fact that became increasingly apparent as the Awami League leadership was excluded by Islamabad from any political solution. If, as Sharp admitted early in the crisis, Islamabad would be able to achieve neither a military victory nor a politically viable withdrawal without first attaining its goals, and if, as Small insisted at the same time, no political leader in East Pakistan could negotiate anything other than extreme autonomy, if not the independence of the East, then a soft policy of influencing Islamabad behind the scenes was extremely unlikely to succeed.

Although Canada preferred to use the carrot in its dealings with Islamabad, it nevertheless had two potential sticks in its armoury. Ottawa was Pakistan's second-biggest source of development aid. . . . However, although a soft policy had little chance of success, a harder policy would also appear unlikely to have succeeded, especially given the ongoing support for Pakistan from two key players on the international stage: China and the US. Each of these major powers continued to back Pakistan throughout the crisis. China, because Pakistan was an ally in Asia, continued to provide political support as well as a US$200 million line of credit to purchase arms. The US, because of Washington's attempts to achieve rapprochement with Beijing, like Canada, refused to condemn Islamabad either publicly or privately, and continued its substantial programme of development aid.

Consequently, while it is very difficult to condone Ottawa's position on moral grounds, it is also hard to see how Canada could have sought to pressure Pakistan into a successful political solution without risking serious damage to the relationship between them, and to no immediate practical avail. Seen in this light, Ottawa's soft policy towards Islamabad, balanced with the need not to unnecessarily sour relations with India, could appear a justifiable option in very difficult circumstances. Nevertheless, it is certainly possible to argue that Canada's broader global interests in the longer term, through the promotion of its human rights and democratic values, would have been better served had Ottawa risked sacrificing its relationship with Islamabad, even if this almost certainly would not have precipitated a viable political solution in East Pakistan.

A Lack of Discussion of Moral and Ethical Issues

Canada made continued efforts to encourage a political settlement and maintain the peace. Ottawa, after some initial hesitation, placed a full embargo on military supplies to Pakistan; in a collective action with others, it voted for the suspension of World Bank aid to Islamabad and it provided humanitarian relief. Trudeau wrote several letters to Yahya and [Indian prime minister] Indira Gandhi imploring them both to act with restraint, and the former to implement a realistic political solution. As war loomed in South Asia, in the absence of a viable UN initiative, Ottawa instructed its ambassador in Moscow to call upon the Soviets to urge restraint in New Delhi. Nevertheless, from the outset, without necessarily knowing that China and the US would develop into such strong supporters of East Pakistan, the dialogue in External Affairs revolved around maintaining Canadian influence in Islamabad in the short, medium and long term. The discussion of moral issues remained disturbingly absent. The only dissenting voice was that of George, who, in raising the matter of ethical considerations, was labelled 'emotional'. As the East Pakistan crisis developed, even Ritchie was forced to admit that the only successful strands of Canadian policy—those of remaining neutral and providing relief aid—combined to treat the symptoms and not the underlying cause. Although it was extremely unlikely that firmer Canadian action would have led to the resolution of the crisis or averted the war, there remained in Ottawa's policy, and in the government's failure to adjust that policy when it clearly was not working, an unfortunate absence of principle and an uncomfortable air of appeasement.

India Forgets the 1971 War and Therefore Judges Pakistan Unfairly

Khurram Hussain

Khurram Hussain is a graduate student in the Department of Religious Studies at Yale University. In the following viewpoint, he argues that India tends to see Pakistan as an Islamic state formed by its roots in Muslim separatism following the end of British rule in 1947. Hussain says that, on the contrary, Pakistan's actions are traceable not to 1947, but to the 1971 civil war, when India helped East Pakistan secede and become Bangladesh. Hussain says that Pakistan's mistrust of India is not irrational but is based on India's actions and on Pakistan's military defeat. He says that this does not justify Pakistan's actions but may help India better understand and work with its neighbor.

On a recent [2009] trip to India, I was moved by the genuine concern people have about Pakistan. As a Pakistani living in the United States, I am subjected daily to serious exasperation, courtesy the American media. Americans do not understand Pakistan because they do not care. And there is no real knowledge without caring. Indians certainly do care. Pakistan has been on the Indian mind since the moment of their co-creation [in 1947, when Britain gave the region its independence]. India and Pakistan are like two ends of a thread tied in a fantastic Gordian knot; their attachment magically survives their severance. And how the love grows! The recent Jaswant Singh controversy over [Muhammad Ali] Jinnah[1] only partially unveiled how Pakistan is critical to the ideological coherence of Indian nationalism in both its secular and Hindutva varieties. But behind this veil, Pakistan has always been internal to Indian politics. It should come as no surprise then that establishment Indians (bureaucratic and political elites, intellectuals, media types, and the chattering classes) are well-versed in the nuances of Pakistani society. Indians understand Pakistan like no one else does, or can.

Forgetting 1971

Still, there is this curious blind spot: no one in India appears to remember 1971 [the year of the East Pakistan conflict]. Worse, no one seems to think it relevant. For all their sophistication, Indian elites continue to understand Pakistan primarily with reference to the events of 1947. Anything else is incidental, not essential. The established Indian paradigms for explaining Pakistan, its actions and its institutions, its state and society, have not undergone any significant shift since the Partition. The tropes remain the same: religion and elite manipulation explain everything. It is as if the pre-Partition politics of the Muslim League [which pushed for an independent Pakistan] continues to be the politics of Pakistan—with slight non-essential variations. More than 60 years on, the factors may be different but little else has changed.

This view is deeply flawed. It reflects a serious confusion about the founding event of contemporary Pakistani society. The Partition has a mesmerising quality that blinds the mind, a kind of notional heft that far outweighs its real significance to modern South Asian politics. The concerns of the state of Pakistan, the anxieties of its society, and the analytic frames of its intellectual

Soldiers stand guard at the Indian Embassy in Kabul, Afghanistan, where a car bomb was detonated in October 2009. The Pakistan secret service is believed to have been involved in the attack because of lingering distrust of India after the civil war. © AP Images/Altaf Qadri.

and media elites have as their primary reference not 1947 but the traumatic vivisection of the country in 1971. Indians have naturally focused on their own vivisection, their own dismemberment; but for Pakistan, they have focused on the wrong date. This mix-up has important consequences.

First, Indians tend not to remember 1971 as a Pakistani civil war, but rather as India's "good" war. It is remembered as an intervention by India to prevent the genocide of Bengalis by Pakistanis. The fact that the Bengalis themselves were also

Pakistanis has been effaced from the collective memory of Indian elites. This makes 1971 merely another Kargil, or Kashmir, Afghanistan or Mumbai—an instance of Pakistan meddling in other people's affairs, and of the Pakistani military's adventurism in the region. This is why mention of Balochistan at Sharm el-Sheikh created such a stir in India.[2] It was literally incomprehensible to Indians that Pakistan could accuse India of meddling in its internal affairs. Surely, this is the pot calling the kettle black. But what the Indian mind perceives as Pakistan's ongoing divorce from reality is in fact Pakistan's most fundamental political reality. The Pakistani establishment has internalised the memory of 1971. In all things, and at all times, it must account for India. Dismemberment has the requisite effect of focusing the mind on existential matters. Nothing can be taken for granted.

Pakistan Is Not Schizophrenic

Second, the Indian establishment routinely misconstrues as ideological schizophrenia the Pakistani intellectual classes' complicated responses to India. The nuances of the Pakistani experience of India are the very picture of incoherence to them. Worse, Pakistanis often frustrate the project of creating a common South Asian sensibility to bridge the political gaps between the two communities.

But again, no one in India accounts for 1971 when making such grand universalising (and, if I may add, genuinely noble) plans for the future of the region. Pakistani intellectual elites share with their Indian counterparts the normative horror of what the West Pakistani military did in the East. How can anyone in their right mind not deem such behaviour beyond the pale? But horror does not preclude abiding distaste for the Indian state's willful opportunism in breaking Pakistan apart. It is for this reason that while the intellectual classes in Pakistan, especially the English language press and prominent university scholars, have almost always condemned their state's involvement in terrorist activity inside India proper, they have remained largely quiet concerning Kashmir [a region in India with a separatist move-ment that Pakistan has supported]. What's good for the goose is good for the gander. Kashmir does not seem so different to them than East Pakistan.

It is for this same reason that there was no great outcry about the isi's [the Pakistan secret service] supposed involvement in the [October 8, 2009] bombing of the Indian embassy in Kabul [Afghanistan]. The general sense among the educated elites was that India deserved it for trying to "encircle" Pakistan through Afghanistan. Indians process this either as paranoia or as a vis-ceral hatred of India that blinds Pakistanis to facts. Perhaps there is some of this too. But it bears appreciating that Pakistan is a post–civil war society. Fear and anxiety concerning India's in-tentions in the region are hardly limited to the so-called 'estab-lishment' in Pakistan. It is a general fear, a well-dispersed fear, a social fear. And a relatively coherent fear at that.

Religion

This leads to the third, and perhaps the most important point. The Indian establishment does not see Pakistan as a 'normal' society. The substance of this abnormalcy is religion, which is also the irreducible difference between the two societies.[3] It is the original sin and a foundational incoherence that is ultimately inescapable. And it has tremendous explanatory power. It ex-plains both the ideological nature of the Pakistani state's hatred of India and, simultaneously, the state's manipulation of the zeal-ous masses for its own ends. That these two explanations do not hold together coherently is besides the point to most Indians. This is an old story and is as such sensible. In the Indian imagi-nation, Pakistan is endlessly regurgitating the politics of Jinnah and the erstwhile Indian Muslim League. While Indian politics moves on, Pakistan's holds eerily still. I am certainly not one to deny that there are some obvious asymmetries between India and Pakistan. The nature of the relationship between religion and politics is certainly one of them. But it bears mentioning

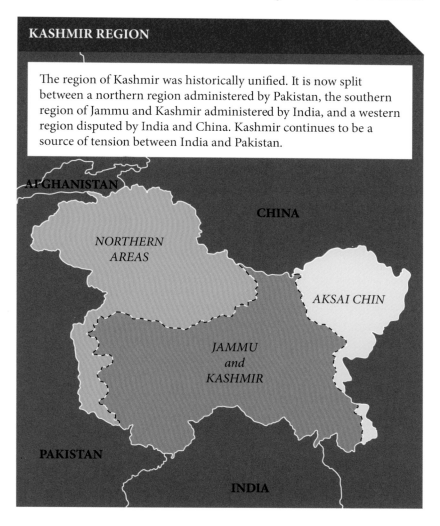

KASHMIR REGION

The region of Kashmir was historically unified. It is now split between a northern region administered by Pakistan, the southern region of Jammu and Kashmir administered by India, and a western region disputed by India and China. Kashmir continues to be a source of tension between India and Pakistan.

AFGHANISTAN

CHINA

NORTHERN AREAS

AKSAI CHIN

JAMMU and KASHMIR

PAKISTAN

INDIA

that perhaps the most relevant asymmetry concerns the repeated defeats suffered by the conventional Pakistani forces at the hands of their Indian counterparts. This asymmetry is neither that complicated nor particularly abnormal. It illuminates the actions of the Pakistani state as essentially strategic and only incidentally ideological. And in that sense, it allows an interpretation of Pakistan as a fairly pedestrian, even 'normal' post-conflict society in its relations with its much larger neighbour.

Ultimately, this is the real value of a renewed focus on 1971 rather than 1947. It normalizes Pakistan. It allows for discussion of real differences between the two societies and the two states, rather than of reified stereotypes that have little political relevance any more. This is not to justify the actions of the Pakistani state, which are in many cases entirely unjustifiable on both moral and political grounds. It is merely to hope that a mutual comprehension of normalcy may lead to peace and progress. Certainly, no one will deny that there is value in that.

Notes

1. Author and politician Jaswant Singh wrote a controversial biography of Pakistan's founder Jinnah, in which he said that Jinnah was not solely to blame for the 1947 partition.
2. At a summit in 2009, Pakistan issued a statement suggesting that India was encouraging a separatist movement in the Pakistani province of Baluchistan.
3. Pakistan is primarily Muslim; India is primarily Hindu.

Pakistan Must Remember and Acknowledge Its Crimes of 1971

Kamran Asdar Ali

Kamran Asdar Ali is an associate professor of anthropology at the University of Texas at Austin. In the following viewpoint, he remembers the history of Bangladesh, including the struggle for greater autonomy from Pakistan and the atrocities of 1971. Ali admits that there were attacks by Bangladeshis upon minority groups in 1971 and says that Bangladeshis must acknowledge this. However, he says that the violence from rioting pales in comparison to the deliberate military attack upon civilians and democratic institutions launched by Pakistan in 1971. He says that Pakistan needs to apologize for the atrocities of 1971 in order to heal relations between Pakistan and Bangladesh.

The just ended month of March [2011] reminds us of many dates in our [Bangladesh's] national history. March 23 is our national day when, in 1940, the Pakistan Resolution was presented by AK Fazlul Haq (Sher-e-Bangla), the same person who later became the chief minister of East Bengal, after the United

Front routed the Muslim League in the March 1954 elections.[1] This ministry was summarily dismissed in May, following ethnic and labour riots in East Bengal. Accusing the government of encouraging radical and anti-state elements, the Karachi-based [that is, based in the former Pakistan capital] political apparatus declared emergency, banned the Communist Party of Pakistan and sent Major General Iskandar Mirza to Dhaka [in East Pakistan] to impose Governor's rule.

Bangladesh's History

If the language struggle of February 1952 [in which activists tried to get the Bengali language recognized as an official language of Pakistan] was the first step, the dismissal of the United Front government made it clearer to a large percentage of East Pakistanis, that the West Pakistani elite was not willing to treat the province as an equal partner. The Awami League's (AL) six points in the 1960s[2] were a continuation of this sentiment of deprivation, inspired as they were by the United Front's earlier demands for autonomy and parity. These six points asked for the supremacy of legislature, for the federal government to only retain defence and foreign affairs, for two freely convertible currencies (to safeguard against flight of capital from East Pakistan), for the authority to collect revenue by the provinces (the federal government would get its share), for two separate foreign accounts and, finally, for the right of provinces to raise their own militia. There was also a call for moving the naval headquarters to East Pakistan. This was not a secessionist argument, rather it was a response to the political maltreatment by West Pakistan, and a call for autonomy and equity, much in accord with the Pakistan Resolution itself.

In the December 1971 elections, the Awami League emerged as the largest party, and it had to be invited to form the government and initiate the process of constitution-making. Rather, between January and March of 1971, the ruling military junta twice postponed the dates for convening the National Assembly.

It also started an incessant drive to portray the six points as a conspiracy to break up the country. It is ironic to note that the regime had earlier permitted the Awami League to conduct its campaign for an entire year on these very points. Somehow they became a problem after AL's victory in the most fair and free elections held in the country.

This brings me to another date, March 26, the national day of Bangladesh. This past week was the fortieth anniversary of that dreadful night of March 25, 1971. Lest we forget, this night saw the most brutal of violence unleashed by a standing army on its own citizens. The horror of that night, when many Bengali intellectuals, academics, students, political workers and common people were killed, is an unwritten and unremembered part of our history. This was followed by nine months of continued killings, rapes and general mayhem, further alienating the East Bengali population from a solution that could have kept Pakistan together.

In official circles, this violence was justified to maintain the nation's integrity. The path taken did not save the country from the ensuing death, destruction and subsequent division, along with the humiliation of surrender in December of 1971. The only viable route was to convene the National Assembly session and respect the will of the people by handing power to the majority party. The Assembly could have voted for autonomy or secession, but it would have shown a democratic and peaceful way out of the impasse.

An Apology Is Needed

Another reason given for this intervention was to stop the killing of non-Bengalis. There is no denying that killings, rapes and other atrocities were perpetrated on non-Bengalis in East Pakistan, in early March. Many lost their lives in Chittagong, Saidpur, Dinajpur, Mymensingh and other places across East Bengal (even my own relatives). However, we also need to understand that the postponement of the assembly session, which was

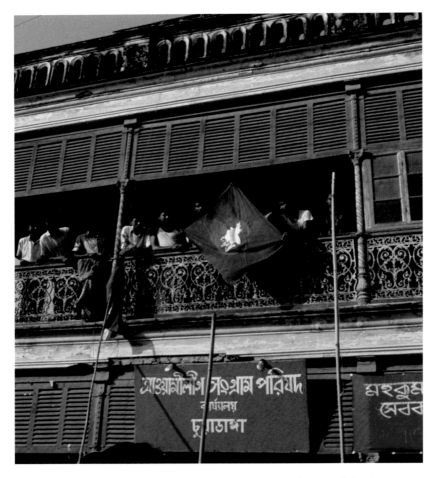

Awami League party members wave the flag of Bangladesh at their party's headquarters in 1971. The party campaigned for the secession of Bangladesh from Pakistan. © Bettmann/ Corbis.

scheduled for March 3, had generated a lot of anger and angst among the Bengali populace who read this as a blatant denial by the West Pakistani governing elite of their right to form government. Archival material has shown that the then Governor of East Pakistan, Admiral SM Ahsan—one of the most decent and honourable public servants this nation has known—had earlier warned Islamabad that if the assembly session was postponed a second time, it would lead to widespread disturbances, including ethnic violence. Rather than heed his warning, Admiral Ahsan was summarily dismissed and relieved of his post on March 1, 1971. As the intellectual Eqbal Ahmed wrote in 1971, clearly the saving of civilians was not the motive for intervention as the killings went on for three weeks prior to March 25, while the generals were seeking extra-parliamentary solutions to the crisis. On the contrary, the subsequent military action clearly increased the killing of Pakistani citizens (mostly Bangla-speaking), and also made millions cross the border into India as refugees fleeing the horror that had been unleashed in their homes. Indeed, every life is sacred, yet killings by vigilantes and excesses by political workers, cannot be morally equated to the actions of a state and an organised and professional military sworn to protect its own citizens.

Rather than blame a politician or an individual, we need to clearly comprehend how a non-elected military regime acted criminally against its own people in a moment of supreme national crisis. Collectively, we need to acknowledge this moment in our history, a period that has been systematically erased from national discourse and popular memory. A further and important issue is one of apology to the people of Bangladesh for the atrocities perpetrated by the Pakistani state machinery during 1971. During a recent visit to Dhaka, to attend a workshop on 1971, Bangladeshi colleagues acknowledged the atrocities committed on the non-Bangla speaking population during this period. The workshop also made evident that the Bangladeshi national history is by itself a contested terrain, yet the pain still lingers, the wound has yet to heal. Where is our acknowledgement of our past? Taking responsibility for the infliction of widespread trauma in 1971, along with an apology by the Pakistani state to the people of Bangladesh, may finally start a healing process, perhaps for both sides. It may also sensitise us to the horrors of war and destruction and make us adhere to the principle of 'never again'.

Notes

1. The United Front wanted greater autonomy for East Pakistan; the Muslim League did not.
2. The Awami League was a party that pushed for greater autonomy for Bangladesh; the six points was its program for autonomy.

Bangladesh's War Crime Trials Are Necessary for Justice

Syed Badrul Ahsan

Syed Badrul Ahsan is the editor of the Daily Star, *a Bangladesh daily newspaper. In the following viewpoint, he argues that war crimes trials in Bangladesh are necessary to bring criminals to justice. He says that Bangladesh became an independent nation in March 1971, and any Bangladeshis who collaborated with Pakistan after that point are essentially traitors. He says that Pakistani officers who committed war crimes in Bangladesh should be prosecuted even if they cannot be extradited from Pakistan and even if they are dead. He concludes that intellectuals who argued on behalf of Pakistan in 1971 and so aided the atrocities should also be prosecuted by the war crimes tribunal.*

These are galvanising times. And yet a degree of caution must be in place as we go through them, indeed as we try to fashion them to our moral and intellectual expectations. All these expectations are wrapped around the tribunal that is now finally in place for a trial of the war criminals of 1971. The central idea here is one of a dispensation of justice. It is not and has never

In recent years, many Bangladeshi citizens have called for the prosecution of war crimes committed against their people by the Pakistani army in the 1971 war. © AP Images/Pavel Rahman.

been one of vengeance. Those who today speak of a witchhunt in the name of war crimes are carefully trying to divert the course of justice and subvert the need for ethics in politics.

Holding to Account

Let the basics of the war crimes trial be clearly understood by all, despite everything that the old war criminals and their sympathisers may try to put across. And the basics are simple: bringing the collaborators of the Pakistan occupation army to trial will certainly not be an effort to embarrass those political parties which have within their fold a good number of these old believers in Pakistan. As for the Jamaat-e-Islami [a pro-Muslim political party in Pakistan], the process of the war crimes trial will not be a persecution of the party but a holding to account of its prominent figures guilty of venality back in 1971.

Three Residents of Great Britain Suspected of Participation in 1971 Genocide

There are three men resident in the UK since the 1970s suspected of direct criminal liability for war crimes committed in the 1971 Bangladesh genocide. . . .

The three are currently London-based, and alleged to have been leading figures in a paramilitary death-squad complicit in the killing of 3 million and systematic rape of up to 400,000 in the closing days of Bangladesh's War of Liberation against West Pakistan.

Testimony this year by a former activist of a political grouping indicted in the 1990s for war crimes alleges one 'infamous collaborator'—who absconded to London in 1971—was 'Operation-in-charge' for the drawing up of lists and killing hundreds of members of the Bengali intelligentsia.

Nizar Manek, "'Impunity Gap'; Straw's Cut-Off Date to Prosecuting War Criminals," OurKingdom, *September 14, 2009.* www.opendemocracy.net.

The tribunal and with it the country ought to be forewarned. Many or perhaps all of the men hauled up for trial as war criminals will in all likelihood try impressing us with the thought that in 1971 they were defending the state of Pakistan as citizens of Pakistan. For these men, the war of liberation remains a 'civil war' in which 'East Pakistan' needed to be defended from the 'secessionists' who sought to destroy Pakistan in the name of Bangladesh.

It is an argument that must speedily be reduced to smithereens, for reasons that are as clear as daylight. And this is the argument the tribunal and the people of Bangladesh can put forth if these collaborators speak of their defence of Pakistan: with effect from March 26, 1971, when the independence of Bangladesh was proclaimed by Bangabandhu Sheikh Mujibur Rahman [the leader of Bangladeshi independence and the first president of Bangladesh]—an act subsequently reinforced by Major Zia's announcement on Bangabandhu's behalf on March 27 as also by the Proclamation of Independence by the Mujibnagar government in April 1971—the state of Pakistan ceased to exist in these parts and the Pakistan army quickly turned into a foreign occupation force. In simple terms, the local Bengali collaborators were, after March 26, waging war against their own people in defence of a foreign state.

One Hundred and Ninety-Five Officers

The tribunal, the prosecution, indeed the Bangladesh state must make note of several other significant factors as the time draws closer for the war crimes trial to commence. The most important one is the need to reopen the files against the 195 Pakistani military officers who were allowed to go home as part of a tripartite deal among Bangladesh, India and Pakistan in the early 1970s. These 195 officers were never pardoned by Bangabandhu's government and so can today be prosecuted by the state of Bangladesh. It is eminently possible that the government of Pakistan will not agree to have these officers extradited to Bangladesh for trial. Even so, the Bangladesh government can officially make an announcement relating to the trial of these 195 officers; and if they are not physically present in Dhaka [capital of Bangladesh], they can be tried in absentia.

What matters in the end is a judicial acknowledgement, on the part of the war crimes tribunal, that these officers of the Pakistan army along with their Bengali collaborators willfully and with little sense of shame or guilt carried out the genocide of three million Bengalis in 1971. The objective will be two-fold here: the Pakistani war criminals, now aging (with some already dead), will officially and legally be stigmatised for their criminality in

1971, and the local Bengali collaborators will of course have their comeuppance for their role in killing, in assisting the occupation army to kill, in raping women, in pillaging during the course of the nine-month war.

Those Bengalis who take the stand as war criminals will in all probability attempt to shift responsibility for their acts on the Pakistan army, which is why the files on the 195 officers should be reopened. The credibility of the trial will certainly go up a good many notches if the likes of Yahya Khan [president of Pakistan in 1971], Tikka Khan [martial law administrator of East Pakistan in 1971], A.A.K. Niazi [commander of Pakistani forces in East Pakistan in 1971] and their fellow officers are also placed in the dock. The fact that many of the Pakistani officers as well as some Bengali war criminals are no more alive ought to be no reason not to try them, posthumously, for what they did in Bangladesh in 1971. The death of a war criminal can be no reason for him to escape public censure.

There is one final point. In the nine months leading up to Bangladesh's emergence in December 1971, a number of right-wing Bengali politicians, academics, journalists and others vociferously defended the Pakistan army's actions in occupied Bangladesh. They did not take part in the killing but they were complicit in helping the Yahya Khan junta implement its genocide programme in this country. These men, dead and alive, should also come into the prosecution net.

Let the wheels of justice roll.

Bangladesh's War Crime Trials Are Politically Motivated and Unjust

Abdul Jalil

Abdul Jalil is a professor in the Department of Business Adminis-tration at International Islamic University in Malaysia. In the fol-lowing viewpoint, he argues that the war crimes trials in Bangladesh are politically motivated. He says that the Awami League (AL) government is using the trials to prosecute members of the rival Islamic Jamaat party. Jalil says that the war crimes tribunals are not up to international standards. He also argues that Jamaat party members should be prosecuted only for war crimes, not for opposing Bangladeshi independence in 1971. He says Jamaat is a democratic party that loyally supported Bangladesh independence since the end of the war. He also argues that the AL government is corrupt and has killed political enemies extrajudicially. He suggests that the war crimes tribunal will be a continuation of AL's unjust policies.

According to national and international press reports, the present Awami League (AL) government[1] in Bangladesh has been oppressing opposition political party leaders and their supporters as a means of revenge against them since it assumed in power in January 2009. So far it has killed more than 200 people extra-judicially and arrested more than 1200 leaders and supporters of Jamaat-e-Islami Bangladesh (Jamaat) [a Muslim party] and Shibir [an Islamic student organization] without any valid reason and they are being oppressed in detention since February 2010. This [viewpoint] mainly focuses on the war crimes trial issue in Bangladesh for war crimes committed in 1971 during independence movement in Bangladesh. . . . It critically explains the *mala fide* [bad faith] intention of the AL government in prosecuting and arresting some of the opposition political party leaders in Bangladesh for their alleged role in 1971.

Roots of Political Conflict

In 1947 Pakistan was created from India after a long struggle and the sacrifice of people who participated in the liberation movement against the UK. Pakistan consisted of two parts: West Pakistan and East Pakistan (known as Bangladesh). Pakistan as a federal country continued its political activities till 1971 when the people of Bangladesh under the Awami League (AL) started a separation movement for certain reasons, such as disparity in development in two parts, declaring 'Urdu' language as the only national language of Pakistan when in fact it was the minority language of Pakistan and not recognizing the national election result which was held in 1971.

Jamaat-e-Islami Bangladesh (Jamaat) opposed the separation of Bangladesh from Pakistan in 1971 along with other five political parties but history proves that it was not involved in any war crimes, such as killing of people, rape, torture of freedom fighters etc. Even many people in Bangladesh say that the supporters of united Pakistan, for example Jamaat, gave shelter to freedom fighters in their houses during the day time so that Pakistani soldiers could not find them out. It just peacefully protested against the separation of Bangladesh for certain good reasons as explained below. However, Pakistan failed to maintain its integrity and surrendered to the Indian Army on 16 December 1971 and on this day Bangladesh became an independent country.

In 1973 during the AL regime, thousands of people were arrested for alleged war crimes, such as assisting the Pakistani army, killing freedom fighters, committing rape, arson and looting. At that time, the AL government identified only 195 people as war criminals after collecting evidence against them. Those suspects were all Pakistani army officers. It is a historical fact that no Jamaat leader or any of its supporters was on the war criminal list.

These 195 Pakistani soldiers who were identified as war criminals were given amnesty and repatriated to Pakistan following a tripartite treaty between Bangladesh, India and Pakistan (known as the Bangladesh-India-Pakistan Agreement, 1974). Before this tripartite agreement another agreement was made, named the Indo-Pak Joint Agreement in 1973. India and Pakistan promised in this agreement to repatriate 195 war criminals to Pakistan. Before that the Shimla Agreement 1972 was made between India and Pakistan with a promise to end the conflict between the two countries and resolve the issue of war prisoners.

The political background of Jamaat in Bangladesh needs to be explained briefly because the AL government has targeted Jamaat leaders to punish them for alleged war crimes committed 39 years ago. The people of Bangladesh are asking why the AL government did not try and punish Jamaat leaders during 1972–1975 and 1996–2001 when they were in power as the government of Bangladesh. Jamaat sources say that 95% of Jamaat supporters were in fact freedom fighters and supporters of freedom fighters during the separation movement in 1971. At present Jamaat is one of the largest political parties in Bangladesh and the AL government is afraid of it. It is known to the Bangladeshi people that AL cannot form government alone, it needs support from Jamaat but Jamaat is not willing to form coalition government with AL because of ideological differences. So, to persecute Jamaat leaders with a political and *mala fide* motive, AL government has already formed the War Crimes Tribunal and appointed prosecutors and judges for the tribunal on 25 March 2010. Now it wants to arrest some of the top Jamaat leaders to prosecute them for war crimes although they were not involved in war crimes in 1971 as explained above. Hence, the question is: What is the real intention of AL government in trying the top leaders of Jamaat in 2010 after 39 years of independence of Bangladesh?

Jamaat Is a Democratic Party

According to BBC news (30 June 2008), Jamaat claims to be a "moderate Islamic political party that believes in democracy and human rights". Jamaat leader Barrister Abdur Razzak said that Jamaat is the victim of a political vendetta. None of its leaders has been prosecuted for the last 39 years for their alleged activities of war crimes during the war in 1971 and the accusations against them seen in the newspapers are baseless and politically motivated. . . .

It is historical fact that Jamaat strongly supports democracy, because in Islam no one has the right to lead a society unless he or she is an elected representative of the people. This is precisely the reason why for more than half a century Jamaat has been following a democratic path. It has participated in almost all the national and local elections. To attain its objectives, Jamaat has never resorted to violence or unconstitutional means. It has always abided by the laws of the country and in the face of extreme provocation and political persecution it defended its rights through legal means. It never adopted or resorted to destructive political means although other political parties in Bangladesh adopted such destructive means to achieve their political goals such as arson, vandalism, fighting with arms, nationwide indefinite strike etc. . . .

Allegations of War Crimes Against Jamaat Leaders

On 16th December 1971, the Pakistani Army surrendered in Dhaka with 93,000 soldiers and they were taken as prisoners

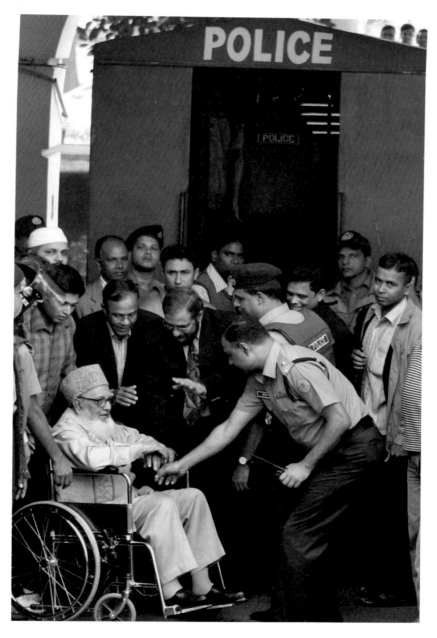

Jamaat-e-Islami party members have recently been prosecuted for alleged war crimes committed during the 1971 war for Bangladeshi independence. Former Jamaat chief Ghulam Azam (seated) is escorted to jail in Dhaka, Bangladesh, in January 2012. © AP Images/Pavel Rahman.

of war (POWs). Out of that number, there were allegations of war crimes against only 195, and they were identified as war criminals by the Government of Bangladesh. On 19th July 1973, the Parliament of Bangladesh passed the International Crimes (Tribunal) Act 1973 to try the alleged war criminals.

It should be mentioned that the Tribunal under the International Crimes (Tribunal) Act 1973 (Bangladesh) has jurisdiction to try and punish any one who was a member of any armed, defense or auxiliary forces and who has committed war crimes or crimes against humanity. According to Jamaat sources, no leaders or members of Jamaat had ever been a member of any armed, defense or auxiliary forces. Therefore, the question of trying them under the Act does not arise. As a matter of fact a Tribunal formed under the International Crimes (Tribunal) Act 1973 has no jurisdiction to try any member of Jamaat because of the clear statement in the Act that its objective is to try and punish 'persons who were members of any armed, defense or auxiliary forces'.

Recently, the Home Minister of Bangladesh openly ordered the Police Department to annihilate the Jamaat and Shibir (a student organization of Jamaat) in Bangladesh. Such an order by the senior Minister of Bangladesh was very unfortunate, discriminatory, unjust, oppressive and autocratic. The people of Bangladesh cannot expect anything good from such a government for the socio-economic and political development of Bangladesh. The whole move of the AL government so far interpreted by the international community as nothing but an extreme political vendetta intended to subdue the opposition parties. . . .

Jamaat's Support of Pakistan in 1971 Was Not Treason

Jamaat was not the only political party that supported the cause of a united Pakistan. At that time there were other five political parties along with Jamaat who opposed the separation movement. Besides these political parties, there were thousands of scholars and intellectuals including university professors, doctors, engineers, journalists and religious leaders who also opposed the separation of Bangladesh from Pakistan and this fact is known to the people of Bangladesh. According to Jamaat sources, they thought that Pakistan had been formed from India by a long struggle and a lot of blood and sacrifice of many people against the English colonial regime and the Indian Congress Party. So, separating Bangladesh with the help of India into two parts would mostly benefit India by allowing her to dominate both the Pakistan and Bangladesh. It was thought by the people of Bangladesh that India could declare Bangladesh as a province of India by force since 65,000 [soldiers in the] Indian army fought in Bangladesh against Pakistan during separation movement. Anyhow after the 9 months war between the Pakistan government and the Bangladesh Freedom Fighters, the Pakistani Army surrendered and Bangladesh became an independent country on 16 December 1971.

It is widely acknowledged by Bangladeshi people that after Bangladesh was separated from Pakistan, Jamaat leaders cordially supported the independence of Bangladesh and its supporters worked sincerely to protect the independence and sovereignty of Bangladesh and did not maintain any links with the Pakistani government. Since the independence of Bangladesh Jamaat leaders have been working for the welfare of Bangladesh and have been very committed to preserve its sovereignty although some other political parties seem not so sincere and committed to preserve its independence and sovereignty.

Violation of Human Rights of Jamaat Leaders

It is very unfortunate that leaders of a few political parties and a section of the press in Bangladesh in a malicious and revengeful campaign labeled the top leaders of Jamaat as 'war criminals'. This is contrary to all civilized norms and the provisions of local and international human rights legislations and the concept of justice. It is a paramount principle of law that a person is presumed innocent until he is proven guilty by a competent court of law. Hence, before labeling Jamaat leaders as war criminals there must be adequate witnesses and other evidence to prove the case beyond reasonable doubt. It is really surprising that although no leader of Jamaat was listed among the 195 war criminals, they have been termed as war criminals with the motive of political persecution. This is a violation of principles of natural justice and also violation of the fundamental rights and human rights of Jamaat leaders which are guaranteed in the Constitution of Bangladesh and a number of International Conventions including the Universal Declaration of Human Rights and International Covenant on Civil and Political Rights.

A Muslim party alliance in the U.S. known as American Muslim Taskforce on Civil Rights and Elections (AMT) organized a press conference on 23 March 2010 in the U.S. They have submitted a memorandum to Ms. Hillary Clinton, the Secretary of State of the U.S. In this memorandum, they mentioned that the Bangladesh government (AL) has become very oppressive to opposition political party members and thousands of them have been killed and wounded. In 2009, 180 people have been killed while in the custody of the law enforcement agency without any trial.

They also stated in the memorandum that no Jamaat leader was convicted of war crimes and collaboration with Pakistan Army between 1972–1975, but the AL government with political *mala fide* motive to destroy Jamaat organization, is planning to try top Jamaat leaders for war crimes and collaboration without any evidence. It is to be noted that many AL supporters also worked as collaborators (Razakar [paramilitary forces]) of Pakistani Army but they are not prosecuted.

AMT told Hillary Clinton that the people of Bangladesh are facing great danger because of democratic and human rights violations, interference with the judiciary, and the collapse of law and order. Government students named Satro League are seriously assaulting and oppressing thousands of opponent political party students in hundreds of universities and colleges all over the country and killing some of them. The education environment in the country is in serious danger. So, the AMT sought the intervention of the U.S. government to put pressure on the Bangladesh government to stop all types of atrocities and political attacks and killings. . . .

The International Crimes (Tribunal) Act of 1973

According to Jamaat central body, Jamaat leaders are not afraid of the 1973 Act or of the trial under the Act. They are in fact afraid of the bias and *mala fide* political motive of the AL Government to hang certain high profile Islamic political figures as a means of political revenge without proving adequate evidence against them. According to Jamaat, such a conspiracy against Jamaat leaders has been planned by the present government. Jamaat leaders are worried that they may not get a fair trial in the Tribunal under 1973 Act and may not get the fundamental constitutional right to appeal against the decision of the Tribunal to the High Court Division or Appellate Division of the Supreme Court of Bangladesh to challenge the decision of the Tribunal.

In April 2009, the Bangladesh government sought assistance from the UN on how to try war criminals in Bangladesh. Renata Lok Dessallien, the Head of the United Nations in Bangladesh said that they would like to assist Bangladesh by providing the names of international war crimes experts so that Bangladesh may conduct the trial fairly and impartially and does not make any mistake.

United Nations (UN) and Human Rights Watch Asia (HRWA) asked the AL Government to modify the 1973 Act so that it conformed with international standards but AL government has failed to do so. HRWA Director Mr. Brady also observed that the International Crimes (Tribunal) Act 1973 had many defects. It was not of international standard. It could not ensure a fair trial and justice. Some innocent people might be victims under this law.

Section 23 of the International War Crimes Act 1973 (The 1973 Act) has taken away basic human rights of the alleged war crimes accused which is guaranteed in the Constitution, Code of Criminal Procedure 1898 and other laws in Bangladesh. It also violates human rights and procedural safeguards provided in the Universal Declaration of Human Rights and the International Covenant on Civil and Political Rights. In June 2009, a delegation from the European Union Troika visited Bangladesh and the press of Bangladesh asked the leader of the Troika delegation Ms. Helena Bambasova some questions regarding the trial of alleged war criminals in Bangladesh under the 1973 Act. In reply she said, "EU thinks that every war crime should be investigated but it has to be done properly, carefully, fairly and transparently". . . .

Politicization and Revenge

The first Prime Minister of Bangladesh Sheikh Mujibur Rahman (the father of the present Prime Minister Sheikh Hasina) declared an amnesty for all the people who were involved in war crimes or collaborated with the Pakistani Army during his rule between 1972–1975. His intention was that the people of Bangladesh wanted independence of Bangladesh and that was achieved. So, the next task was to unite the people from all parties and to take their assistance to develop the war-torn country. To develop the country, assistance is needed from all the opposition political parties. That was a great political philosophy of the father of the present Prime Minister of Bangladesh.

The separation movement happened 39 years ago and it is normal that some people may oppose the separation of a country into two parts as happened in Bosnia, Russia, India etc. However, the people who are involved in war crimes, genocide, rape etc. must be tried and punished as soon as possible. For the case of Bangladesh it was not done, rather the 195 Pakistani soldiers who were convicted as war criminals were forgiven and repatriated to Pakistan under a three country agreement in 1974 and collaborators were given amnesty in 1975 as stated above.

The present government after 39 years has reopened the settled chapter to punish the war criminals, but it is very difficult to get adequate evidence to find the accused guilty after 39 years because most of the eye witnesses have died or become so old that their memory does not work properly and many of the documentary evidence has been destroyed or lost. The accused cannot be convicted and punished merely based on newspaper information which AL government wants. This will work contrary to the fundamental principle of criminal law and law of evidence that 'the offence must be proved beyond reasonable doubt' to convict an accused. Besides, AL government wants to try and punish only top Jamaat leaders (who claim that they were not involved in war crimes) although more than five political parties and thousands of independent intellectuals and scholars opposed the separation movement as stated earlier in my discussion. This is not fair to try the leaders of one political party only while declaring amnesty to other political party leaders who also committed the same offence. This is known as politicizing the event and taking revenge of an opponent political party which is getting good support from people for its democratic and social activities.

Prominent lawyers of Bangladesh have protested against the International War Crimes Tribunal which has recently been established by the AL government in Bangladesh and said this Tribunal is illegal. They have questioned the validity of the International War Crimes (Tribunal) Act 1973 (Bangladesh). They also questioned the impartiality and integrity of the judges, investigation committee and the prosecution team appointed under this Act, because they are all hardcore supporters of the present government. They said that most of the sections of the 1973 Act are contrary to the Constitution of Bangladesh, Penal Code, Code of Criminal Procedure and the evidence Act of Bangladesh. Article 102 of the Constitution of Bangladesh gives right to appeal and judicial review to the High Court Division and Appellate Division of the Supreme Court of Bangladesh, but this Article has been excluded by the 1973 Act with a political *mala fide* motive.

The present AL government won at the general election held on 29 December 2008 where it got majority seats at the Parliament. Before the general election, the party promised to reduce the price of daily necessary things including fertilizer and rice; to create employment opportunities for unemployed people by setting up new industries, to attract foreign investment, to stop corruption and terrorism, to solve the problem of electricity deficiency which is a serious problem in Bangladesh where temperature is between 35 to 40°C in summer season, to give primary education to hundred percent children in the county etc. Instead of spending precious time on the settled issue on war crimes, the government should work hard to fulfill the promises given to the people before election and to satisfy the people so that this government can win in the next general election again.

Note

1. The political party that led the independence movement in 1971.

CHAPTER 3

Personal Narratives

Chapter Exercises

1. **Writing Prompt**

   Imagine you are a Bangladeshi in 1971 when the Pakistan army enters East Pakistan. Write a one-page diary entry describing your experiences and thoughts.

2. **Group Activity**

   Form groups and develop five interview questions that could be used in conducting oral histories of the experiences of Biharis in Bangladesh during the 1971 crisis.

A Bangladeshi Civilian Describes the Events of March 1971

Jahanara Imam

Jahanara Imam was a Bangladeshi writer and political activist. The following viewpoint reproduces her diary entries at the beginning of the East Pakistan conflict in March 1971. Imam recalls the excitement of demonstrations in Dhaka in favor of Bangladeshi independence and the anxiety and fear as West Pakistan began its military response. She also remembers her fear that West Pakistan had a much superior military force and would use it to crush dissent in East Pakistan. She recalls hiding evidence of her family's support for independence and hearing gunshots from the university, where the West Pakistan military attacked students.

It is Resistance Day today [March 23, 1971]. Early in the morning we all went to the roof to hoist the black flag and the new flag of independent Bangladesh. It was a mixed feeling of joy, excitement, expectation, apprehension, fear and uncertainty.

Flying a New Flag

After breakfast we drove along the streets of the city. The black flag and the new flag, bright in green, red and yellow were flying

Jahanara Imam, *Of Blood and Fire: The Untold Story of Bangladesh*. New Delhi, India: Sterling Publishers Private Limited, 1989, pp. 34–42. Copyright © 1989 by Sterling Publishers Private Limited.

on every house top. We took some pictures. We stopped at Banka's house at road No. 2, Dhanmondi. From there we went to Dr. Khaleque's house just opposite Banka's house. There we met Dr. Khaleque's sister-in-law Madira and her husband, a retired Commander of the Pakistan Navy, Moazzem Hussain. After retirement Moazzem formed a political organisation two years ago entitled "Lahore Resolution Implementation Committee." Whenever I met Moazzem in the past he always said, "Sheikh Mujib[1] has six-point demands but, I have only one; that is the independence of Bangladesh."

Today Moazzem said: "Sheikh has also now been compelled to accept the one point."

"How's that?"

"This morning he himself had to hoist the flag of independent Bangladesh in his own house."

Mrs. Khaleque asked: "Did you go to see the parade at Paltan?"

"No, we only drove along the streets and saw lots of new flags. All the office buildings have also raised the flag of independent Bangladesh, even Hotel Intercontinental."

"How could they do it in the presence of so many senior army officers?"

Moazzem said, "Bengal is unconquerable, so are the minds of the Bengalees."

"Even the foreign missions are flying the new flag. It was a touching sight at the "Shaheed Minar,"[2] the pillars are covered with fantastic posters drawn by Qamrul Hasan. There is a satanic face drawn on each poster which looks very much like that of Yahya Khan. Underneath there is the caption 'Finish them.'"

"Is that so? We must go and see." . . .

Disturbing News
Thursday, 25th March, 1971

After the remarkable success of the Resistance Day on 23rd March, there was a shadow of gloom. Only disturbing news came from everywhere. The meetings between Yahya, Mujib and Bhutto[3] failed to find a solution. Sheikh Mujib carried on his meetings with the President and after the meetings continued to repeat to the journalists that the talks were progressing. At the same time he asked the people to carry on with their struggle. He called upon them to build fortresses in every house.

For the last few days there have been rumours afloat that thousands of Pakistani troops were landing at Dhaka airport in plain clothes. I didn't want to believe it but still it created a sense of unease in me. Some friends telephoned from Chittagong and informed us that shiploads of weapons have arrived from West Pakistan. The Bengalee porters of the port refused to unload this cargo and built barricades on the streets. To prevent them the army shot at them at random.

There is a two-day-old stubble on Rumi's unshaven face. Clutching a handful of his hair, he said: "You know Mother, the Mujib-Yahya talks are bound to fail. It is only a Pakistani ploy to gain time. They will never give us independence on a platter. We will have to win it through armed struggle."

I shuddered. "What are you talking about? The Pakistani army has got all the latest weapons. What would you fight them with?"

In an excited voice Rumi replied, "Exactly, I fully agree with you. Sheikh Mujib is going to the President House everyday in his white car flying the black flag, but there is no progress in the talks. Meanwhile, thousands of Pakistani troops are landing in plain clothes at the airport and ships loaded with weapons are anchoring at Chittagong port. At the same time the so-called Bengalee heroes armed with bamboo staves are marching to Bangabandhu's [that is, Sheikh Mujibar] house to salute him. After returning home they have a feast of rice and fish and take a siesta with the satisfaction of having done their duty. At the Paltan grounds, they are parading with dummy rifles. Are we still living in a land of fairy tales? There must be a limit to naivety."

"What is the solution then?"

"I don't see any, Mother."

A cold wave of fear and terror ran down my spine. "No, no. Don't say that. You are saying it only because you don't support Sheikh's political moves. You hot blooded young people are itching for a fight. Sheikh is guiding the movement in the right direction. Even if the talks with Yahya fail, the non-violent, non-cooperation movement will lead us to our goal."

"Mother, you are still living in a fool's paradise. Just look at these few facts—whatever has happened in East Pakistan is directed against the Pakistani Central Government. In normal times these would have been considered acts of high treason. The President of the country is in Dhaka but East Bengal is following the directives of Sheikh Mujib. Offices, courts and banks do not obey the Government. They obey Sheikh. Then look at the humiliation of the Pakistani government. Tikka Khan could not become the governor because no judge agreed to give him the oath. He had to be satisfied with the post of Martial Law Administrator. The President landed in Dhaka and there was a demonstration in front of his house. No Bengalee is selling any foodstuff to the armed forces any more. They are virtually surviving on bread and water. They even had to get food from West Pakistan by plane. In the face of acts of such defiance the Yahya government has been extremely tolerant. Don't you see why? They are only buying time. These discussions are nothing but eyewash. The Sheikh is too late. This is not the way of survival."

I was getting impatient. I said, "Go shave and take a cold shower. That will cool you down." Rumi quietly got up to go to his room. I was quite demoralised, as if I had lost all strength.

Tonight we have an invitation for dinner at Atiq and Bulu's place. Both husband and wife are Tagore song artistes [a Bengalese song form named for Rabindranath Tagore]. I was not in a mood for dinner. At the same time it was suffocating to stay

Photo on previous page: The feelings of joy and excitement demonstrated by Bangladeshi people on Resistance Day were echoed when Sheikh Mujibur Rahman returned from exile in January 1972. Crowds celebrated his return by waving flags in Dhaka, Bangladesh. © Bettmann/Corbis.

at home. Sharif had to attend a meeting at the Dhaka club and so I went alone. There I met Enayetullah Khan and his wife Lina, Lina's brother Zillur Rahman and his American wife, Margaret. Also present were Atiq's friend Halim and his wife Moni, Atiq's brother-in-law, Fattah, and his wife Tulu. The same question was on everybody's lips, "What's going to happen?" . . .

Gunfire

I was fast asleep. Suddenly I woke up at a very loud sound. Rumi and Jami came rushing to our room. "What's the matter?" Deafening sounds of heavy guns, the intermittent sounds of machine guns, the whistling sound of bullets filled the air. The tracer balloons brightened the sky. We all ran up to the roof. South of our house, across the playground, are the University Students' dormitories—Iqbal Hall, Mohsin Hall and a few other buildings of the University quarters. All the noise came from that direction. There were screams of anguish and heartrending cries of the victims along with the sound of weapons. We could not stay there for long because of the sparks. Rumi quickly lowered the black flag and that of independent Bangladesh.

Suddenly I remembered that Barek and Kasem were in the outhouse on the ground floor. We all rushed down. As soon as we opened the wooden door to the courtyard our alsatian dog Mickey rushed in and started moaning pathetically and rolling on the ground. I called Barek and Kasem. They came in quickly, I told them to bring their beds and sleep in the drawing room.

Mickey refused to move out of the room. It seemed that all the noise of the guns and the light of the tracer balloons had badly shaken him. Rumi lovingly patted his head and said: "Don't be afraid, Mickey. You will stay with us upstairs." But he refused to go upstairs either. He was looking for a corner. Finally he crept into a dark corner under the staircase and curled up quietly there.

I lifted the receiver. The phone was dead. Hearing Baba's voice, Rumi was holding his hands and telling him something in a whisper.

There was no sleep for the rest of the night. I went upstairs again. There was fire visible at a distance. We could still hear the sound of different types of guns, big and small. The tracer balloons continued to inflame the sky. There were sounds of people crying for help all around. The pillars of fire were getting bigger and higher in the North, South, East and West.

Nobody uttered a word. Rumi and Jami opened up the polythene packets and unloaded the contents into the commode, a little at a time lest it got blocked, and then pulled the flush. Jami washed the mortars and pestles very carefully with dish-washing powder to remove the smell of chemicals.

After that, Rumi packed all his books on [communist writers Karl] Marx, [Friedrich] Engels as well as [Chinese communist leader] Mao Tse Tung's military writings into a polythene bag. We did not know where to keep them. We didn't want to bury them underground because it would spoil the books. Then I remembered a gap between Barek's room and the boundary wall. We threw the packet of books in there as soon as the faint light of dawn appeared on the horizon. Rumi covered the packet with a few dried fronds of palm.

Terror on Every Face
Friday, 26th March 1971

At six o'clock in the morning I heard a faint voice calling me. I ran to the window and looked out nervously. I saw Kamal Ataur Rahman, curled up under a tree in the garden. Kamal is an Honours student at the Dhaka University and stays in the Mohsin Hall. I rushed down and opened the door. Rumi and Jami helped me to bring the semi-conscious Kamal indoors. He had spent the night with a few other students in a bathroom in the Hall. Due to the bright tracer balloons he did not dare to come out at night. As soon as the morning light appeared they all left the bathroom and fled in different directions.

After some nursing and breakfast, Kamal felt a little better. We switched on the radio. After recitation of the Holy Quran only one piece of music was being played over and over again—the instrumental rendering of a popular patriotic song. At 7 o'clock in the morning, I went to our neighbour, Dr. A.K. Khan's place to use their telephone but it was also dead. Gradually some more faces appeared at the windows of our neighbourhood. There was terror on every face. Everybody had spent the night awake and nobody knew what was really happening. All the telephones were dead.

I returned and kept sitting in front of the radio, I told Jami, "Go wake your grandfather up. Wash him and feed him with the help of Barek."

Kasem left the breakfast tray on the table like an automaton. Nobody touched any food.

At 9 o'clock, the instrumental music suddenly stopped and a harsh voice was heard on the radio. Curfew was announced all over the city until further orders. People were also reminded of the punishment for violating curfew. Martial law was announced and all the articles of the martial law were read out. The announcements were made in Urdu [the official Pakistani language] first and then in English. The pronunciation, style and accent betrayed the Army background of the announcer. Probably the military government could not find any more suitable person at this time.

Curfew for an indefinite period! Even without curfew nobody would dare to go out amidst the shootings and firings. There was no end to the sound of the gun shots. The pillars of fire were getting bigger and bigger and now we could see them from our windows. The dark smoke covered a large part of the bright blue sky over the city.

Mickey continued his moaning all morning. His alsatian nature had been changed by the sound of non-stop gun shots. We all in turn tried to cheer him up and feed him but to no avail.

Baba was another problem. We had a hard time explaining to him why the Pakistani troops were killing the innocent people. I was afraid that his blood pressure might go up again.

The telephone was dead. The radio station was crippled. There was curfew outside and the unending sound of all types of guns made our lives miserable. There was no way of knowing what was really happening. Under the circumstances the only first hand information could be obtained from Kamal Ataur Rahman. From the morning he has been repeating his story to satisfy my curiosity.

"What were you doing at 12 o'clock at night, Kamal?"

"I was writing an essay on Patriotism in Bengalee literature. I was going to read it on the radio on the 27th."

"When did you first hear the gun shots?"

"At around midnight. A friend of mine came and told me: 'You are still here! Don't you know what's happening all around? The soldiers are coming to attack our campus. I am leaving. You better do the same.' But we never had a chance to leave. The firings started almost immediately thereafter. As soon as the sky was brightened with the tracer balloons the firings increased. From my room on the 5th floor I quickly came down to the ground floor. On the south of Mohsin Hall is the Iqbal Hall and the Muslim Hall is next to it. It appeared as if the heavy guns were pounding the Iqbal Hall. Some of the bullets were entering our Hall too."

"Didn't they attack your Hall?"

"No, though we were expecting an attack any moment."

"Where else did they attack?"

"I don't really know. But it appears that the Iqbal Hall, the Muslim Hall, the Jagannath Hall and the Shaheed Minar were the main targets. Most of the sound came from that direction."

"Do you think that they have razed the Iqbal Hall and Muslim Hall to the ground? What about the students, are they all killed?"

"There is no way of knowing. We were hiding in the bathroom in the ground floor. We could hear the noise of window panes shattering all around us the whole night."

When I left Kamal, Rumi told me; "Don't ask him any more, Mother. Can't you see it hurts him to repeat his nightmarish experience?"

"I can see that. But I want to know what is happening."

"There is nothing to know Mother, whatever was to happen has happened."

I looked deep into Rumi's eyes. He lowered his gaze. He has become somewhat quiet and withdrawn since last night I remembered Rumi's prediction—it had finally come true.

Rumi must have been thinking, "Didn't I tell you? Have you at last been thrown out of fool's paradise?"

The Whistle of Bullets

How long could one stay indoors under such conditions? I opened the door and went to the porch. The road in front of our house [is] in a cul-de-sac. Branching out from the Elephant Road it ends just beyond our house. There is an advantage of a blind alley, because there is very little traffic. Sometimes we neighbours talk to each other on the road. It is like a common courtyard. Since the house was built in 1959, we would spend time chatting on our road every time there was a curfew. But today I did not dare to step out of the porch. I could still hear the whistle of the bullets. I could hear dogs barking and people screaming—a very faint sound from a distance. Or was it my imagination? Could people still be alive and cry for help after such a shower of lead? Surprisingly, all the birds have disappeared. I could not even hear a crow.

I peeped over the boundary wall and looked at the main road. There was no sign of any life there. Had I continued to stare I could probably have seen truck loads of troops passing by. But I had no interest in them. The house opposite ours belongs to Mr. Hussein. I could see him moving restlessly from his chair in the drawing room to the door and then to the verandah and then to the chair again. On the left is Dr. Rashid's house. He was also moving between the front room and the verandah nervously. As I turned back, I caught sight of that sticker on the rear window of the car—'Each letter of the Bengali alphabet represents one of us'.[4] I asked Rumi to take off the sticker immediately.

Just before evening the electricity went off. Our cup of misery was full to the brim. There was some respite in the sound of gun shots. Mickey also appeared somewhat more composed. He went out and sat on his favourite wooden box on the left of the courtyard. He also ate some food.

I took out some candles and lit them. I placed them at different places on the ground floor and the top floor. Barek and Kasem have stayed indoors the whole of today. In the evening I told them to bring their beds into the guest room and asked them not to go out into the courtyard at night. Gratefully, they brought their beds inside. I felt as if we were all sitting in Noah's Ark.

There is not one radio in good condition in the house. On 20th February when we were all out there was a theft in the house and our expensive radio was stolen. After that we were using Kitty's radio. But since she left for Gulshan we have been managing with Rumi and Jami's little portable two-in-one. It is hard to get the BBC [British Broadcasting Corporation] on it. All India Radio has so far only said that there are troops on the streets in Dhaka and nothing more. Dhaka TV station is closed. There was nothing to do and so we had early dinner. As we were leaving the dining room, Rumi suddenly remarked: "Mickey is rather quiet. Looks like he has finally overcome the shock."

Jami said: "We should bring him inside."

We opened the door and went to the courtyard. In the flickering candlelight we saw Mickey lying in the courtyard. He was dead.

Notes

1. Sheikh Mujibar Rahman, leader of the movement for Bangladesh autonomy.
2. The Shaheed Minar is a national monument in Dhaka, Bangladesh, in honor of those killed during demonstrations in 1952.
3. Yahya Khan, president of Pakistan; Sheikh Mujibar Rahman, leader of the movement for Bangladesh autonomy; and Zufikar Ali Bhutto, leader of an important Pakistani political party.
4. Support for the Bengalese language was linked to support for Bengalese autonomy.

An American Witness Describes Bengali Attacks on Biharis

Anonymous

An American engineer in East Pakistan describes how ethnic Bengali mobs rioted in favor of independence. The engineer says that mobs indiscriminately attacked Biharis—non-Bengali Muslims—killing them and burning their homes and stores. He says that Bengali mobs were whipped into frenzy by propaganda radio broadcasts. He says that after they killed all known Bihari men, they came back to attack women and children and those suspected of not being born in Bengal. The engineer says that some Bengalis worked to protect Biharis and West Pakistanis, however. He describes the arrival of the West Pakistan army and its efforts to restore order as well as its engagement in unjust killing.

Shortly after March 1 [1971], we received word from some British friends in Chittagong that Bengali mobs had begun looting and burning the homes and businesses of the West Pakistani residents and were beating, and in some cases killing, West Pakistanis as well as Hindus.

"The Events in East Pakistan, 1971: A Legal Study," Secretariat of the International Commission of Jurists, Geneva, 1972. http://nsm1.nsm.iup.edu. Copyright © 1972 by International Commission of Jurists. All rights reserved. Reproduced by permission.

Attacks on Biharis

On the night of March 9, my expatriate staff and I decided to depart Kaptai. As we passed through Chittagong we noted three of four fires. A service station attendant told my driver these were homes and businesses of 'Biharis' [non-Bengalese Muslim residents of East Pakistan].

We returned to Kaptai on March 23. There was a small Army garrison stationed at Kaptai. They were a part of the East African Rifles which was a regiment of Bengalis with mostly Punjabi [a region on the border between India and Pakistan] officers and N.C.O.'s. The garrison was quartered in an old school building about 400 yards from our residences.

On the morning of March 26 around 9 A.M. we heard shooting coming from the school. I went to investigate and found a large crowd gathered there. Some of the crowd was shooting toward one of the upstairs school rooms. I was told that the previous night all Punjabis in the Army garrison (about 26 or 27) had been arrested and locked in the school-room. Now someone in the crowd was claiming that shots had come from the room. After removing a sheet of roofing several men with guns gathered around the opening and began firing into the room. After a few minutes they came down and began dispersing the crowd. I later learned that the commanding officer, who was under house arrest within sight of the school, was slowly beaten and bayoneted to death as his staff was being shot. The officer's wife, in a state of terror, asked the mob to kill her too. She was beaten to death. Their small son was spared and taken in by a Bengali family.

I met immediately with the local Awami League[1] leader and the Power Station Manager, a Bengali named Shamsuddin. The Awami League leader said the people had been told to remain peaceful and that he had peace patrols roaming the area, but that he could not control the large mobs. Shamsuddin told me that the mobs had killed many Biharis the night before and thrown their bodies over the spillway of the dam. He said he just managed to talk the mob out of taking his three West Pakistani engineers but felt they were still in great danger.

Mobs Attack

All India radio began an almost continuous propaganda barrage of East Pakistan. This inflammatory propaganda roused the mobs in Kaptai to new frenzies. After all known Biharis, including at least two of our employees, had been killed, a search was begun for 'imposters'. On about the third day of the trouble we saw two Bengali soldiers marching away a servant who worked in the housing area. A few seconds later we heard a shot and ran out into the road. The servant had fallen partway down a ravine. A crowd quickly gathered and, when it became apparent the servant was still alive, dragged him up onto the road. One of the soldiers motioned the crowd away, knelt and very deliberately fired another bullet into the body. After a short while the death-limp body was dragged and rolled into the back of a pickup and hauled away. It had been found out that although the servant had been living in Kaptai over 20 years, he was born in India. By this time the mobs were killing anyone not a 'son-of-the-soil'.

Friends and acquaintances in Chittagong said that on the night of March 25 Bengali mobs descended on the homes of all known Biharis and especially those military personnel living outside their cantonment. The mobs slaughtered entire families and I heard many horrible descriptions of this massacre. The mutinous East Pakistan Rifles along with irregulars laid siege to the Chittagong military cantonment. After seven or eight days the siege was broken by a relief detachment which had force-marched from the cantonment at Camilla. I am told that when the entrapped garrison broke out it was with a terrible vengeance. The slightest resistance was cause for annihilation of everyone in a particular area. For instance, the Army made a habit of destroying, by tank cannon, everything within a wide radius of hostile roadblocks. I saw the remains of a completely razed three to four square block area of Chittagong near the entrance to the port area. I was told that after encountering resistance here the Army encircled and set fire to the entire area and shot all who fled. Hundreds of men, women and children were said to have perished here.

When the East Pakistan Rifles and Bengali irregulars began retreating from the fighting around Chittagong, many of them passed through Kaptai en route to Rangamati and the Indian border areas. These renegades began looting their fellow Bengalis as they came through Kaptai. They also began to murder the surviving wives and children of previously killed Biharis. They demanded and took food, clothing and other supplies from the local residents. By April 10, everyone in Kaptai, including myself had become terrified of these deserters. Mr. Shamsuddin suggested, and I agreed, that he and several members of his staff, along with families, move into the houses around my residence.

After great pressure from implied threats, Shamsuddin had finally handed his three West Pakistani engineers over to a mob after he was told they would not be harmed, only held in jail at Rangamati. Shamsuddin agreed to hand over the engineers provided two Bengali members of his staff be allowed to accompany the engineers on their trip to the jail. This was agreed and they were taken away. Everyone felt certain these men would be killed but they were spared. When I last heard of them they were safe with their families in Dacca. Shamsuddin, although a Bengali, attempted on several occasions, at great risk to himself and his family, to stop the killings by the mobs but with little success. Also he saw to it that the existing generating units remained in operation throughout the trouble.

The Pakistan Army Arrives

An Army unit arrived in Kaptai on the morning of April 14. Except for those in our area Kaptai and surroundings were completely deserted. The unit consisted of a tank, two jeeps, a half-track and about 250 infantry. As they approached the tank fired blanks from its cannon and the soldiers fired intermittent bursts from their weapons. The object seems to be to lower the inhabitants with the noise. The army immediately began burning the shanties ('bustees') in which most of the people had lived. The bazaar and a few permanent type dwellings were also burned.

While his troops were searching the area, the commanding officer and his staff took tea in our residence. They congratulated and warmly praised Shamsuddin and his staff for their attempts to maintain order and for keeping the generating units in operation. The C.O. said that the Army's objective was to restore normality as quickly as possible. One of the officers told of a terrible scene they had come upon in a town about 10 miles from Kaptai called Chandagborna. About 40 to 50 women and children—survivors of previously killed Biharis—had been taken into a loft building where they had been hacked, stabbed and beaten to death. He said this grizzly scene had driven the troops to an almost incontrollable rage and he said it was fortunate that Kaptai was deserted except for us.

[Mr. Shamsuddin was later taken from the house by two Pakistan soldiers.] We ran after them. They were taken behind the fire station which was about 250 yards away. Just as we arrived at the station we heard two shots. Shamsuddin and another man lay dead on the grass, each with a bullet through his chest.

The officer-in-charge appeared and questioned the soldier who had done the killing. We later found this man was a Major. After questioning by the O.I.C. [Officer in Charge] the Major's weapon was taken and the Major was ordered immediately to Chittagong. The O.I.C. told us the whole thing was a tragic mistake. Later I was told what had happened. While directing the search of the area the Major and his driver came upon a woman with a small child who told that her husband and son had been killed by the Bengalis. She charged that Shamsuddin was the leader of the mobs and instigator of the atrocities. The woman was taken to the fire station and the Major and his aide set off to find Shamsuddin. When Shamsuddin was brought before the woman she immediately identified him and the Major instantly carried out the executions. The man who died with Shamsuddin had also been accused by the woman, who was crazed by fear and grief.

Notes

1. The Awami League was the East Pakistan political party promoting greater autonomy.

A Pakistani Soldier Remembers the Campaign Against East Pakistan

Nadir Ali

Nadir Ali was an officer in the Pakistani army during the East Pakistan conflict; he later became a poet and short story writer. In the following viewpoint, Ali describes the campaign against East Pakistan. He says that he did not commit any atrocities himself, but reports that he was ordered to kill all Hindus, and he knew of numerous incidents in which civilians were murdered by Pakistani soldiers. Ali says that some officers would brag about killing civilians. He says that even though he did not kill anyone, he shares the guilt for having joined the Pakistani army. This guilt contributed to a period of memory loss and insanity that caused Ali to leave the army.

During the fateful months preceding the dismemberment of Pakistan, I served as a young Captain, meantime promoted to the rank of the Major, in Dhaka as well as Chittagong. In my position as second-in-command and later as commander, I served with 3 Commando Battalion.

Kill the Hindus

My first action was in mid April 1971. "It is Mujibur-Rahman's [the political leader of the movement for Bangladesh autonomy] home district. It is a hard area. Kill as many bastards as you can and make sure there is no Hindu[1] left alive," I was ordered.

"Sir, I do not kill unarmed civilians who do not fire at me," I replied.

"Kill the Hindus. It is an order for everyone. Don't show me your commando finesse!"

I flew in for my first action. I was dropped behind Farid Pur. I made a fire base and we fired all around. Luckily there was nobody to shoot at. Then suddenly I saw some civilians running towards us. They appeared unarmed. I ordered "Stop firing!" and shouted at villagers, questioning them what did they want. "Sir we have brought you some water to drink!" was the brisk reply.

I ordered my subordinates to put the weapons away and ordered a tea-break. We remained there for hours. Somebody brought and hoisted a Pakistani flag. "Yesterday I saw all Awami League [the political party supporting Bangladesh autonomy] flags over your village" I told the villagers. That was indeed the fact. I didn't know whether to laugh or cry. Later the main army column caught up to make contact. They arrived firing with machine guns all around and I saw smoke columns rising in villages behind them. "What's the score?" the Colonel asked.

"There was no resistance so we didn't kill anyone," he was informed.

He fired from his machine gun and some of the villagers who had brought us water, fell dead. "That is the way my boy," the Colonel told this poor Major.

I was posted there from early April to early October. We were at the heart of events. A team from my unit had picked up Sheikh Mujib Ur Rehman from his residence on 25th March, 1971. We were directly under the command of Eastern Command. As SSG [Special Services Group] battalion commander, I received direct orders from General [Amir Abdullah Khan] Niazi, General [Yahya] Rahim and later Gen. Qazi Majid of 14 Div Dhaka. . . .

Thousands Killed

I came back to West Pakistan for getting my promotion to Lt. Colonel, in my parent corp, Ordnance, in October 1971. From December 1971 onwards, I began to suffer memory loss till my retirement on medical grounds in 1973. I remained in the nut house for six months in 1973. As a Punjabi [a region on the border between Pakistan and India] writer, I regained my memory and rebuilt my life. I remember every moment from the year 1971.

For operations and visits to my sub units, I travelled all over East Pakistan. I never killed anybody nor ever ordered any killing. I was fortunately not even witness to any massacre. But I knew what was going on in every sector. Thousands were killed and millions rendered homeless. Over nine million went as refugees to India. An order was given to kill the Hindus. I received the same order many times and was reminded of it. The West Pakistani soldiery considered that Kosher. . . .

What drove me mad? Well I felt the collective guilt of the Army action which at worst should have stopped by late April 1971. Moreover, when I returned to West Pakistan, here nobody was pushed about what had happened or was happening in East Pakistan. Thousands of innocent fellow citizens had been killed, women were raped and millions were ejected from their homes in East Pakistan but West Pakistan was calm. It went on and on. The world outside did not know very much either. This owes to the fact that reporters were not there. . . .

All these incidents, often gone unreported, are not meant to boast about my innocence. I was guilty of having volunteered to go to East Pakistan. My brother-in-law Justice Sajjad Sipra was the only one who criticized my choice of posting. "You surely have no shame," he said to my disconcert. My army friends celebrated my march from Kakul to Lahore. We drank and sang!

None of us were in two minds. We were single-mindedly murderous! In the Air Force Mess at Dacca, over Scotch, a friend who later rose to a high rank said, "I saw a gathering of Mukti Bahini [Bangladesh resistance fighters] in thousands. I made a few runs and let them have it. A few hundred bastards must have been killed" My heart sank. "Dear! It is the weekly *Haath* (Market) day and villagers gather there," I informed him in horror. "Surely they were all Bingo Bastards!," he added. There were friends who boasted about their score. I had gone on a visit to Commilla. I met my old friend, then Lt. Col. Mirza Aslam Beg and my teacher, Gen. Shaukat Raza. Both expressed their distaste for what was happening. Tony, a journalist working with state-owned news agency APP, escaped to London. He wrote about these atrocities that officers had committed and boasted about. It was all published by the *Times of London*. The reading made me feel guilty as if I had been caught doing it myself! In the Army, you wear no separate uniform. We all share the guilt. We may not have killed. But we connived and were part of the same force. History does not forgive!

Notes

1. West Pakistanis erroneously believed Hindus were leading the independence movement.

An Indian Civilian Remembers Bangladesh Just After the War

Prakash Subbarao

Prakash Subbarao is the CEO of Spark Consultants, a digital marketing organization in Bangalore, India. In the following viewpoint, he remembers traveling across the border into Bangladesh as a college student in 1972, just after the end of the war. He talks about the wreckage left in the wake of the war, including destroyed bridges and unexploded shells left on the ground. He talks about the tension and anxiety in Bangladesh as Bangladeshi forces rounded up Pakistani fighters and sympathizers. Subbarao recalls almost being mistaken for a Pakistani before his safe return to India.

I have traveled a fair bit in my time but the most exciting journey I have ever made came in early 1972.

I was in Calcutta then, on a holiday during my college vacation. My close friend and neighbour in Bangalore, Naren Udaygiri, was with me.

The Benapole Border

The Pakistani Army Commander in the Eastern Command, Lt. General A. A. K. Niazi, had surrendered to Lt. General Jagjit Singh Aurora of the Indian Army on 16th December, 1971 and Bangladesh had been borne. My father had a lot of contacts with the Government-in-exile of Bangladesh and so I pestered him to take me to Bangladesh.

All one needed in the days immediately after the war was a pass signed by the Indian Army or issued by the Bangladesh Government in Exile which operated from a building in South Calcutta and called itself "Mujibnagar" after Mujibur Rehman [the leader of the Bangladesh independence movement and the first president of Bangladesh].

We got the pass from the Army and on 2nd January set out to see the new country. I took along my mother's camera, a Leica with a Zeus Icon lens. Another hardy piece of equipment that she had purchased in 1958 and which was still going strong in 1972.

My father had told me that we would go to Bangladesh only on one condition—that we would leave very early in the morning and return the same day. In those days it was very dangerous as there were a lot of fleeing Pakistani troops who were still armed and a lot of Razakar's—Bihari [that is, non-Bengalese] Muslim civilians who had supported the Pakistanis' violent suppression of the people of former East Pakistan.

The border is not very far from Calcutta and can be reached fairly quickly. When we got there, there seemed to be some sort of commotion going on. This was at Petrapole, on the Indian side. Apparently a car trying to smuggle guns had been detected by the Indian Army and we were advised that there would be a long delay.

We got out of the car to stretch our legs and to try and work our way out of the jam. We were in luck—there was a Mukti Bahini officer (a Bangladeshi Freedom Fighter), Arun Barun Biswas, who was in a hurry to get to his place and he offered to

Indian army trucks patrol the city of Jessore, Bangladesh, in December 1971, shortly after the war ended. © AP Images.

get us out of the traffic jam and moving if we could drop him at Khulna. We agreed and thereby started a great adventure.

Using his influence we were off in minutes. He knew everyone at the customs. We came to a halt at the Benapole Land Customs on the Bangladesh side which is a little further down the road. There we saw a very young boy, maybe just 15 years old but already a hardened Mukti Bahini fighter standing on guard with a Lee Enfield 303 rifle. The rifle was almost three fourths his height!

We were soon waved through when they saw Arun Barun Biswas with us.

Scenes of Destruction

As soon as we entered Bangladesh, we could feel a strange tension in the air. Everywhere we looked, we saw scenes of destruction. Railway lines torn up, burnt cars and trucks on the side of the roads, buildings bearing bullet holes indicative of the aimless firing of machine guns. . . .

There were no civilians on the streets. Just Indian Army soldiers everywhere.

Just after the border comes the town of Jessore with its Cantonment. It was here that I got my first taste of a war zone.

In their bid to stop the advance of the Indian Army, the Pakistani troops had blown up the bridge and the Indian Army had created a temporary floating pontoon bridge. Huge Army trucks were crossing and had preference and we had to wait till they got across. It was like a scene out of a war movie!

All the buildings were pock marked with bullet marks. There were burnt out petrol stations all along the route.

The road, though a metal one, was rough because it had been churned up by tank tracks.

There were Indian Army 'Shaktiman' trucks patrolling everywhere, with a machine gun mounted on the roof and an alert gunner scanning the area for any disturbance.

A little further we came across a Sherman T-42 Pakistani Army tank that had been abandoned. The machine gun with live ammunition dangling from it was still in the turret! I hopped off the car and stood on the tank and was duly photographed.

A Captured Razakar

I asked Biswas whether he had been a participant in the war in this sector. He said 'yes'. "The Indian Army did not use the roads but traveled off the road, in the fields" he told me. He said that he would show us foxholes where the Pak Army had dug in. We detoured and saw the foxholes. Some of them had suffered direct hits by Indian Air Force aircraft but many were intact.

In one foxhole there was a live unexploded rocket! It would have detonated at the slightest vibration and seeing this made our hairs stand on end in fright. We tiptoed away from it.

A little further we saw a huge group of people standing in the middle of the road. There seemed to be a lot of commotion and we immediately knew that something out of the ordinary was taking place. We stopped the car and elbowed our way forward to see what it was.

A Razakar had been captured!

We saw this bearded person in ethnic dress with his hands tied behind his back being marched by a huge crowd. We were told that they would probably finish him off in the next few minutes. I asked whether I could take a photograph. "Yes" Biswas said and promptly introduced us to the crowd as "international photographers"!!! . . .

Biswas got off in Khulna and we were sorry to see him go. We had lost a good guide and a person who had had firsthand knowledge of the war in this sector.

Almost Mistaken for Pakistanis!

On the way back, I wanted to have a cigarette and so we stopped the car. My friend Naren Udaygiri (sadly no more in this world) and I strolled off the road for a hundred metres or so.

I lit a cigarette.

I suddenly became aware of a group of villagers eyeing us out of the corner of their eye.

"Kya baath hail?" I asked them.

They instantly started slowly creeping upon us the way they would on a wild animal, intent on capturing it. I realized with a shock that they thought we were Pakistani! Hindi [the most common Indian language] and Urdu [the language of Pakistan] are so similar that instead of welcoming me as an Indian they were trying to capture me thinking I was a Pakistani!

"Aami Indian aachee!" (I am an Indian) I told them in broken Bengali. "Aamee Kolkatta thakay aaschee" (I have come from

Calcutta). Aamaar gaadi raastaa thakay aachay!" (My car is on the road). That slowed their advance and they followed us back to the road. When they saw a Calcutta registered Ambassador car (WBG 8537) they relaxed and it was only then that we saw a few smiles. I tentatively offered a hand shake to the headman and he reciprocated warmly. We were now no longer Pakistanis but liberating Indians! They waved as we drove away.

We were soon back at the Indian border. We were actually happy to be back in India. The safety that India exudes is unbelievable and can be felt only after such trysts with danger. We were finally able to let our guard down and relax!

The saddest part of this story is that I lost all the pictures taken on this trip. It happened in Dubai [in 2003]. I was telling some colleagues about the trip and I could see that they felt I was pulling a fast one. I took the pictures to the office to show it to them. There were four or five pictures—me standing on the tank with live ammo, the Jessore bridge in pieces, the Razakar been marched off, hands tied behind his back.

I lost the envelope with the picture in them, a few days later.

With it went the chance of proving the above strange tale.

It is 100% true, I assure you.

A Researcher Interviews Bangladeshi Women Who Were Assaulted in 1971

Sayeeda Yasmin Saikia

Sayeeda Yasmin Saikia is a professor of peace studies at Arizona State University. In the following viewpoint, she reproduces interviews with women who were victimized during the 1971 conflict in East Pakistan. In one case, a Hindu woman whose family supported independence was attacked by her Muslim neighbors. For the rest of her life, Saikia says, the woman was ostracized by her community because of the rape. Saikia also reproduces an interview with a Muslim Bihari (non-Bengalese) woman whose pregnant eighteen-year-old daughter was killed by Bengali neighbors. Saikia says that women have been forced to remain silent about such stories and continue to face systematic oppression in Bangladesh.

The rich feminist literature on 1947 [the year that India and Pakistan gained independence] and my direct encounter with survivors of 1971 have helped me to understand one issue. It is not the women themselves, but the structures and institutions outside their control, that restrict their speech and force them to forget what they endured. Silence serves as a tool to

Sayeeda Yasmin Saikia, "Beyond the Archive of Silence: Narratives of Violence of the 1971 Liberation War of Bangladesh," *History Workshop Journal*, Autumn 2004, pp. 281–283. Copyright © 2004 by Oxford University Press. All rights reserved. Reproduced by permission.

confuse women, and even now, decades later, the women cannot make sense of their horrific experiences nor find answers about why they were targeted in the war that men fought and controlled. The story of Madhumita (name changed) that I quote below illuminates women's experiences during and after the war [of 1971]. Madhumita told me her story in many parts; I quote only two segments of a larger interview that was over six hours long. In her story we hear the voice of a young Bengali Hindu girl who was brutalized and tormented by her neighbours and family friends, who used the occasion of the war to victimize her. We learn from her that after the war her life did not take a better turn, but rather that she was made to pay dearly for her victimization in 1971. Madhumita was, and continues to be, a victim of her own society; the oppression is unending. I met Madhumita in her home. Her elderly mother (around eighty years old) was also present at the first meeting. Madhumita started her story by introducing herself and her family.

Madhumita's Story

I (Madhumita) was fifteen years old and a student of grade VIII in 1971. Ours was a rich Hindu merchant family and we lived in a composite Bengali village. On June 21, 1971, local Bengali and Bihari [non-Bengali Muslim] men of the Muslim League [an Islamic political party], supporters of Pakistan, came to our house. My family used to know them very well. They came to arrest my father and brothers because our family was involved in the liberation struggle and were supporters of the Mukti Bahini [Bangladesh freedom fighters]. But when the Biharis approached our house, all the adult men fled. My youngest brother, who was eleven years old, could not escape. I tried to help him, but was apprehended by the attackers. They locked me in a room; my brother was there too.

At this point of the interview, her mother, who was sitting besides her, broke down and started to wail. Madhumita stopped recounting the details about the horrible night of her victimization. Her mother's wail penetrated the stillness of the room. Her cries were heartrending. I had destroyed whatever peace had existed in the household, and that shook me. But I could not leave. So I sat there and listened to the painful screams of her mother's agony. The pain of remembering what happened on the fateful night was unbearable for her. The old lady slumped and fainted. Then Madhumita's brother came in, and carried his mother out of the room. Our conversation stopped for the day. Several weeks later when I met Madhumita again . . . she began her narrative where she had left off. On this occasion her mother did not join us. Without making direct reference to her experience of sexual violence, Madhumita said,

> After they finished their business they set the house on fire and walked away. But I could not let my brother die. So I dragged myself and despite the pain I was suffering, I helped my brother to escape by breaking open the door. I was badly burned in the process. That night, I hid in our backyard pond. Next morning, when I emerged from the pond chunks of flesh started falling off my body. I had no clothes on, except burned shreds to cover some parts. When I looked around, I saw some men from our village returning from their morning prayers. On seeing me they made funny noises and gestures. I tried to tell them I was not a prostitute but so-and-so's daughter, and tried to solicit their help. But they walked away. Since that day I have been a living dead. My body is in pain. I have no status, job, or education. My brother now owns the family business and I live in his house. I gave up my dignity, my life, everything for my brother; but today I am no better than his servant. This is women's lot in Bangladesh.

Madhumita's voice, like that of many Bangladeshi women, is the voice of a victim. Pride in saving her brother is intricately linked with her own victimization at the hands of her neighbours. In her story we hear that her family's religion and politics provided justification for making her the enemy body. Bengali and Bihari Muslim men under the guise of saving nation and community destroyed her and then left her to die and burn. We almost smell her burning flesh, and can feel her pain as she emerges from the pond to seek help from her neighbours only to be rebuffed and treated ever since as a social outcast. As we listen to her we want to undo the nightmare of that night and inject a measure of normality into her life. Instead, we are left with a sense of her unending loneliness, with no one to share her memories, fears, anxieties or hopes.

An Assault on a Bihari Woman

I spoke with and recorded the testimonies of over fifty victims in Bangladesh during my fifteen months stay. Almost all the women who shared with me their horrific memories of war talked at length about the pain of betrayal inflicted by men they knew— men who belonged, perhaps, to their community, their village, even their family. One Bihari woman recounted the murder of her daughter in 1971.

> [My] daughter's name was Fatima. She was eighteen years old in 1971 and was married. She was expecting her first child in a few months. After the war was over, on March 28, 1972, some Bengali men from [their] neighborhood stormed into [their] mohalla [compound]. They killed Fatima's husband, then they pulled her out of her room into the courtyard. They disrobed her. Then they slit her throat. But that was not enough. They ripped open her stomach, pulled out the unborn child and tore it into two. Fatima died immediately.

Recounting this story was not an easy task for Fatima's mother. She lost her composure many times. But she continued.

> My daughter was innocent. Like all other women in Bangladesh she was like cattle. We are here because our men wanted us to be here. I came to this country because of my husband. He thought he would be better off in East Pakistan, so we came

here in 1957 from India. I never chose to come here, nobody even asked me. No one asked my daughter what she wanted. The Bengalis thought she was an enemy because she spoke Urdu [the official language of Pakistan]. They killed her without showing any mercy. It was not her crime that she was born a Bihari. Has anyone asked us women what we did to deserve this? Has anyone asked a mother how much it hurts to lose a daughter? I am a victim, and I understand what other victims feel. Women are victims in this country. Help us, please, help us. We also deserve to live like human beings.

These testimonies of women shock us, as they should. 1971 was a nightmare; the violence was relentless. The enemy, as women revealed over and over again, was within, not outside. This is why women have been forced to remain silent.

Glossary

Awami League A Bangladesh political party that played a leading role in agitating for independence before and during the 1971 East Pakistan conflict. It remains an active center-left, secular political party in contemporary Bangladesh.

Bangladeshi An inhabitant of Bangladesh.

Bengali (or Bengalese) The major ethnic group in Bangladesh.

Bengali Language Movement A political movement that called for the recognition of the Bengali language as an official language of Pakistan. The language movement began shortly after the formation of Pakistan and made Bengali an official language in 1956. The movement helped inspire the Bangladesh independence movement.

Bihari A minority ethnic group in Bangladesh. In general Biharis sided with the West Pakistanis during the 1971 conflict. Many of them were denied citizenship following Bangladeshi independence and remain stateless.

East Pakistan The eastern wing of Pakistan from 1947 to 1971. After the 1971 war, East Pakistan became independent Bangladesh.

Kashmir The northwestern region of the Indian subcontinent. Parts of Kashmir are administered by India, parts by Pakistan, and parts by China. Control of Kashmir has long been a major source of conflict between India and Pakistan.

Mukti Bahini Bangladeshi combatants who fought for independence during the 1971 East Pakistan conflict. The Mukti Bahini included Bangladesh civilians and soldiers. Most of the Mukti Bahini were ethnic Bengalis.

Operation Searchlight The 1971 Pakistani military offensive against East Pakistan. It resulted in numerous atrocities.

Pakistan Peoples Party An important political party in Pakistan.

Six Point Movement A Bengali nationalist movement led by Sheikh Mujibur Rahman that agitated for greater autonomy for East Pakistan.

West Pakistan The western wing of Pakistan from 1947 to 1971. After the 1971 war, West Pakistan and East Pakistan split, with West Pakistan becoming modern-day Pakistan.

Organizations to Contact

American Institute of Pakistan Studies (AIPS)
University of Wisconsin, Department of Anthropology
5420 Social Science Building
1180 Observatory Drive
Madison, WI 53706
(608) 262-5696
e-mail: aips@pakistanstudies-aips.org
website: www.pakistanstudies-aips.org

AIPS is a nonprofit educational organization whose mission is to encourage and support research on issues relevant to Pakistan. It also works to promote scholarly exchange between the United States and Pakistan. It publishes the *Annual of Urdu Studies* and *Pakistaniaat*, an academic journal that focuses on Pakistani history, culture, and literature.

Amnesty International
5 Penn Plaza, 14th Floor
New York, NY 10001
(212) 807-8400 • fax: (212) 463-9193
e-mail: aimember@aiusa.org
website: www.amnestyusa.org

Amnesty International is a worldwide movement of people who campaign for internationally recognized human rights. Its vision is of a world in which every person enjoys all of the human rights enshrined in the Universal Declaration of Human Rights and other international human rights standards. Each year it publishes a report on its work and its concerns throughout the world. Amnesty International's website includes numerous reports and news items about human rights in Pakistan and Bangladesh.

Carnegie Endowment for International Peace (CEIP)
1779 Massachusetts Ave., NW
Washington, DC 20036
(202) 483-7600 • fax: (202) 483-1840
e-mail: info@ceip.org
website: www.ceip.org

CEIP is a private, nonprofit organization dedicated to advancing cooperation between nations and promoting active international engagement by the United States. It publishes the quarterly journal *Foreign Policy*, a magazine of international politics and economics that is published in several languages and reaches readers in more than 120 countries. Its website includes numerous news articles and publications, including many focusing on Pakistan.

Gendercide Watch
Suite #501, 10011 - 116th Street
Edmonton, Alberta
Canada T5K 1V4
e-mail: office@gendercide.org
website: www.gendercide.org

Gendercide Watch seeks to confront acts of gender-selective mass-killing around the world. It works to raise awareness of such acts and reduce stereotypes and reprisals against victims. Gendercide Watch conducts research, provides educational resources, and maintains a website. The website includes an extensive series of cases studies, news releases, and other information pertaining to gendercide.

Human Rights Watch
350 Fifth Ave., 34th Floor
New York, NY 10118-3299
(212) 290-4700 • fax: (212) 736-1300
e-mail: hrwnyc@hrw.org
website: www.hrw.org

Founded in 1978, this nongovernmental organization conducts systematic investigations of human rights abuses in countries around the world. It opposes discrimination against those with HIV/AIDS. It publishes many books and reports on specific countries and issues as well as annual reports and other articles. Its website includes discussions of human rights and international justice issues, including many focusing on human rights and war crimes tribunals in Bangladesh.

Institute for the Study of Genocide (ISG)
John Jay College of Criminal Justice
899 Tenth Ave., Room 325
New York, NY 10019
e-mail: info@instituteforthestudyofgenocide.org
website: www.instituteforthestudyofgenocide.org

The ISG is an independent nonprofit organization that exists to promote and disseminate scholarship and policy analyses on the causes, consequences, and prevention of genocide. To advance these ends, it publishes a semiannual newsletter and holds periodic conferences; maintains liaison with academic, human rights, and refugee organizations; provides consultation to representatives of media, governmental, and nongovernmental organizations; and advocates passage of legislation and administrative measures related to genocide and gross violations of human rights. In addition to newsletters, the ISG publishes books on the topic of genocide such as *Ever Again? Evaluating the United Nations Genocide Convention on Its 50th Anniversary and Proposals to Activate the Convention* and *The Prevention of Genocide: Rwanda and Yugoslavia Reconsidered.*

International Criminal Court (ICC)
PO Box 19519, 2500 CM
The Hague, The Netherlands
+31 (0)70 515 8515 • fax: +31 (0)70 515 8555

e-mail: visit@icc-cpi.int
website: www.icc-cpi.int

The ICC is a treaty-based international court established to try perpetrators of the most serious crimes of concern to the international community. Its website includes annual reports on the activities of the court, information about situations and cases, relevant legal texts, and other information.

Montreal Institute for Genocide and Human Rights Studies (MIGS)
Concordia University
1455 De Maisonneuve Blvd. West
Montreal, Quebec, H3G 1M8 Canada
(514) 848-2424, ext. 5729 or 2404
fax: (514) 848-4538
website: http://migs.concordia.ca

MIGS, founded in 1986, monitors native-language media for early warning signs of genocide in countries deemed to be at risk of mass atrocities. The institute houses the Will to Intervene (W2I) Project, a research initiative focused on the prevention of genocide and other mass atrocity crimes. The institute also collects and disseminates research on the historical origins of mass killings and provides comprehensive links to this and other research materials on its website. The website also provides numerous links to other websites focused on genocide and related issues, as well as specialized sites organized by nation, region, or case.

Prevent Genocide International (PGI)
1804 S Street, NW
Washington, DC 20009
(202) 483-1948 • fax: (202) 328-0627
e-mail: info@preventgenocide.org
website: www.preventgenocide.org

PGI is a global education and action network established in 1998 with the purpose of bringing about the elimination of genocide. In an effort to promote education on genocide, PGI maintains a multilingual website for the education of the international community. The website maintains a database of government documents and news releases, as well as original content provided by members.

STAND/United to End Genocide
1025 Connecticut Ave., Suite 310
Washington, DC 20036
(202) 556-2100
e-mail: info@standnow.org
website: www.standnow.org

STAND is the student-led division of United to End Genocide (formerly Genocide Intervention Network). STAND envisions a world in which the global community is willing and able to protect civilians from genocide and mass atrocities. In order to empower individuals and communities with the tools to prevent and stop genocide, STAND recommends activities from engaging government representatives to hosting fundraisers, and has more than one thousand student chapters at colleges and high schools. While maintaining many documents online regarding genocide, STAND provides a plan to promote action as well as education.

United Human Rights Council (UHRC)
104 N. Belmont Street, Suite 313
Glendale, CA 91206
(818) 507-1933
website: www.unitedhumanrights.org

UHRC is a committee of the Armenian Youth Federation. The UHRC works toward exposing and correcting human rights violations of governments worldwide. The UHRC campaigns against violators in an effort to generate awareness through boycotts, community outreach, and education. The UHRC website focuses on the genocides of the twentieth century.

United States Department of State
2201 C Street, NW
Washington, DC 20520
(202) 647-4000
website: www.state.gov

The US Department of State is the agency of the federal government responsible for foreign affairs. The website includes daily press briefings, reports on policy issues, and numerous other articles. The office of the historian (http://history.state.gov) includes historical diplomatic documents, including those relating to the 1971 East Pakistan conflict.

List of Primary Source Documents

The editors have compiled the following list of documents that either broadly address genocide and persecution or more narrowly focus on the topic of this volume. The full text of these documents is available from multiple sources in print and online.

The Blood Telegram, April 6, 1971

A diplomatic cable sent by US diplomat Archer Blood that strongly denounced the United States' pro-Pakistan policy.

Congressional Record, September 8, 1971

Senator Edward Kennedy outlines his findings and recommendations from his visit to the refugee camps in India. He praises India and criticizes US policy.

Convention Against Torture and Other Cruel, Inhuman, or Degrading Punishment
United Nations, 1974

A draft resolution adopted by the United Nations General Assembly in 1974 opposing any nation's use of torture, unusually harsh punishment, and unfair imprisonment.

Convention on the Prevention and Punishment of the Crime of Genocide
(General Assembly Resolution 260), December 9, 1948

A resolution of the United Nations General Assembly that defines genocide in legal terms and advises participating countries to prevent and punish actions of genocide in war and peacetime.

Hamoodur Rahman Commission Report, October 23, 1974

A report commissioned by the president of Pakistan following the loss of the 1971 war. Headed by chief justice of Pakistan Hamoodur Rahman, it accuses Pakistani generals of atrocities, corruption, and incompetence.

Indira Ghandi's Radio Speech, December 3, 1971

The prime minister of India declared war on Pakistan. The speech was reprinted in the *New York Times* on December 4, 1971.

Mujibur Rahman Speech, March 7, 1971

Sheikh Mujibur Rahman, leader of the Bangladeshi independence movement, rallied the Bangladeshis for an independence struggle. The speech is sometimes referred to by its most famous phrase, "This time the struggle is for our freedom."

Principles of International Law Recognized in the Charter of the Nuremburg Tribunal
United Nations International Law Commission, 1950

After World War II (1939–1945) the victorious allies legally tried surviving leaders of Nazi Germany in the German city of Nuremburg. The proceedings established standards for international law that were affirmed by the United Nations and later court tests. Among other standards, national leaders can be held responsible for crimes against humanity, which might include "murder, extermination, deportation, enslavement, and other inhuman acts."

Rome Statute of the International Criminal Court, July 17, 1998

The treaty that established the International Criminal Court. It establishes the court's functions, jurisdiction, and structure.

United Nations General Assembly Resolution 96 on the Crime of Genocide, December 11, 1946

A resolution of the United Nations General Assembly that affirms that genocide is a crime under international law.

Universal Declaration of Human Rights
United Nations, 1948

Soon after its founding, the United Nations approved this general statement of individual rights it hoped would apply to citizens of all nations.

Whitaker Report on Genocide, 1985

This report addresses the question of the prevention and punishment of genocide. It calls for the establishment of an international criminal court and a system of universal jurisdiction to ensure that genocide is punished.

For Further Research

Books

M. Rafique Afzai, *Pakistan: History and Politics 1947–1971*. New York: Oxford University Press, 2001.

Donald W. Beachler, *The Genocide Debate: Politicians, Academics, and Victims*. New York: Palgrave Macmillan, 2011.

S.K. Bhattacharyya, *Genocide in East Pakistan/Bangladesh: A Horror Story*. Houston, TX: A. Ghosh, 1988.

Sarmila Bose, *Dead Reckoning: Memories of the 1971 Bangladesh War*. New York: Columbia University Press, 2011.

W. Norman Brown, *United States and India, Pakistan, Bangladesh*, revised edition. Cambridge, MA: Harvard University Press, 1973.

Syed Shahid Husain, *What Was Once East Pakistan*. New York: Oxford University Press, 2010.

Adam Jones, *Crimes Against Humanity: A Beginner's Guide*. Oxford, UK: Oneworld, 2008.

William B. Milam, *Bangladesh and Pakistan: Flirting With Failure in South Asia*. New York: Columbia University Press, 2011.

William van Schendel, *A History of Bangladesh*. New York: Cambridge University Press, 2009.

Jaswat Singh and S.P. Bhatia, *Conflict and Diplomacy: US and the Birth of Bangladesh*. New Delhi, India: Rupa & Co., 2008.

Richard Sisson, *War and Secession: Pakistan, India, and the Creation of Bangladesh*. Berkeley: University of California Press, 1990.

Stanley A. Wolpert, *India and Pakistan: Continued Conflict or Cooperation?*. Berkeley: University of California Press, 2010.

Periodicals and Internet Sources

Khaled Ahmed, "Analysis: Pathology of Gradual Fall," *The Friday Times*, vol. 23, no. 45, December 23–29, 2011. www.thefridaytimes.com.

Maqbool Ahmed, Syed Zahid Ali, and Shamsuddin Ahmad, "Famine and Civil War in East Pakistan," *The Lancet*, vol. 298, no. 7732, November 6, 1971, pp. 1029–1030.

Julhas Alam, "Bangladesh Wrestles with Trials From '71 War," *San Francisco Chronicle*, December 21, 2011. www.sfgate .com.

BBC News, "Bangladesh War Crimes Trial Begins in Daka," November 20, 2011. www.bbc.co.uk.

BBC News, "Nixon's Dislike of 'Witch' India," June 29, 2005. www.bbc.co.uk.

Sarmila Bose, "Anatomy of Violence: Analysis of Civil War in East Pakistan in 1971," *Pakistan Think Tank*, November 4, 2010. http://pakistanthinktank313.wordpress.com.

Chester Bowles, "Pakistan's Made-in-USA Arms," *New York Times*, April 18, 1971.

Tom Cooper with Khan Syed Shaiz Ali, "India-Pakistan War, 1971; Introduction," *ACIG*, October 29, 2003. www.acig.org.

Simon Dring, "Dacca Eyewitnesses: Bloodbath Inferno," *Washington Post*, March 30, 1971.

Mark Dummett, "Bangladesh War: The Article That Changed History," BBC News, December 15, 2011. www.bbc.co.uk.

Gendercide Watch, "Case Study: Genocide in Bangladesh, 1971," n.d. www.gendercide.org.

Faheem Haider, "Bangladesh and Pakistan in Nicholas Kristof's Bent View," Foreign Policy Association, May 21, 2010. http://foreignpolicyblogs.com.

Peter R. Kahn, "Grieving Multitudes Flee East Pakistan, Add to Area's Turmoil," *Wall Street Journal*, April 28, 1971.

Nicholas D. Kristof, "Pakistan and Times Sq.," *New York Times*, May 12, 2010. www.nytimes.com.

James Melik, "Bangladesh at 40: The Challenges Ahead," BBC News, December 15, 2011. www.bbc.co.uk.

Nittin Pai, "Remembering the East Pakistan Genocide," *The Acorn*, March 25, 2008. http://acorn.nationalinterest.in.

Sanskar Shrivastava, "1971 India Pakistan War: Role of Russia, China, America, and Britain," *The World Reporter*, October 30, 2011. www.theworldreporter.com.

Time, "The World: East Pakistan: Even the Skies Weep," October 25, 1971. www.time.com.

Times of India, "US Envoy Says Bangladesh Needs Fair War Crimes Trial," November 28, 2011. http://timesofindia .indiatimes.com.

John E. Woodruff, "Pakistan Is Exterminating the Bengalis," *Baltimore Sun*, April 4, 1971.

Other

Bangladesh Genocide Archive (www.genocidebangladesh .org) An online archive of documents, video, eyewitness accounts, and other resources pertaining to the 1971 genocide in Bangladesh.

The *Daily Star* (www.thedailystar.net) This newspaper is a prominent Bangladeshi English language daily. Among its news articles are many that relate to the history and legacy of the 1971 war.

India-Pakistan Conflict Hub, GlobalSecurity.org (www.global security.org) GlobalSecurity.org is a public policy organization that provides news and analysis focusing on defense and security issues. The India-Pakistan Conflict Hub includes analysis and extensive historical background on the tensions between India and Pakistan.

Index